edited by
ANTHONY SLIDE

From *My Three Sons* to *Major Dad*

My Life as a TV Producer

Filmmakers Series, No 118

John G. Stephens

THE SCRARECROW PRESS, INC.
Lanham, Maryland · Toronto · Oxford
2005

SCARECROW PRESS, INC.

Published in the United States of America
by Scarecrow Press, Inc.
A wholly owned subsidary of
The Rowman & Littlefield Publishing Group, Inc.
4501 Forbes Boulevard, Suite 200, Lanham, Maryland 20706
www.scarecrowpress.com

PO Box 317
Oxford
OX2 9RU, UK

British Library Cataloguing in Publication Information Available

Library of Congress Cataloging-in-Publication Data

Stephens, John G., 1929–
    From My Three Sons to Major Dad: my life as a TV producer / John G.
Stephens.
        p. cm. — (Filmmakers series)
    Includes index.
    ISBN 0-8108-5279-9 (pbk. : alk. paper)
    1. Stephens, John G., 1929–. 2. Television producers and directors—
United States—Biography. I. Title. II. Series.
PN1992.4.S79A3 2005
791.4502'33'092—dc22   2004013777

∞™ The paper used in this publication meets the minimum requirements of
American National Standard for Information Sciences—Permanence of Paper
for Printed Library Materials, ANSI/NISO Z39.48-1992.

Manufactured in the United States of America.

For my late wife, Joan, our son, Bill,
and our daughter, Laurie,
who shared these times with me.

Contents

Preface

Who is John Stephens? What has he done? Who does he know and what does he know about them? Was he a part of television from the mid-1950s through the early 1990s? Did he give Aaron Spelling his first writing job? Did he get Charles Bronson and Angie Dickinson their first leading television roles? Has he worked with Fred MacMurray, Barbara Stanwyck, and Henry Fonda? Did he work with Jimmy Stewart and Katy Jurado at scale and fire Ethel Merman? Was he responsible for getting *60 Minutes* on the air during prime time? Did he rub elbows with John Forsythe, Brian Keith, Betty White, Eva Marie Saint, Daniel Mann, James Wong Howe, Zsa Zsa Gabor, Frank Tashlin, Howard Koch, Jo Van Fleet, William Frawley, James Arness, Don Bellisario, Don Fedderson, Dick York, and Robert Altman? The answer is yes!

I had a project going with Brandon Tartikoff during Brandon's first week as head of NBC. I almost ruined the careers of Ryan O'Neal, Nick Nolte, and Ron Howard. I listened to Brian Keith tell me to "fire Garry Marshall because he doesn't understand humor." I created *Major Dad* and left the show because it was boring. At Universal, I had a show in the top five and a show in the bottom five at the same time! After watching a young actress read for a pilot, I remarked, "She's very pretty, but she can't act." That was Halle Berry.

Most books written about TV or the movies concern themselves with other people's mistakes, but this book is different. I made what is arguably the worst ninety-minute TV movie of the week that ever aired, the original *Wonder Woman* pilot with Cathy Lee Crosby. I also made three movie of the week pilots that were so bad they never aired.

In reading this book, you'll become acquainted with the people involved with and the working of the hit shows *The Millionaire*, *My Three Sons*, *Family Affair*, *Gunsmoke*, *How the West Was Won*, *Simon & Simon*, and *Major Dad*. You'll also get the inside story on a number of failures and learn about the B movie days and two-day TV shows.

There are two major changes in the way the industry works today from how it used to work. First, authority is mostly in the hands of the stars. If your show is a hit, be prepared for your stars' salaries to escalate. In the 1990s, the stars of the hit situation comedy *Friends* demanded outrageous salaries, and the network buckled. Back in 1959, on the hugely popular show *The Millionaire*, Marvin Miller was receiving $750 per episode. Marvin played the character of Michael Anthony, who opened every show by taking a check from billionaire John Beresford Tipton and delivering it to that week's recipient. He was indispensable to the show, or so he thought. Marvin went up to see Don Fedderson, the owner of Don Fedderson Productions.

"Don, my salary is ridiculous. I'm the star of this show. The guest stars are making more than I am."

"Marvin, your contract says $750 for seasons six and seven."

"I know, but Don, I think—"

"I'll do the thinking, Marvin. Your salary stays at $750 per episode for the next two seasons. If you're unhappy, we'll replace you. Anything else you want to discuss?"

"No, Don. You can't blame me for trying, can you?"

"A deal's a deal, Marvin."

Let's get one thing straight about the youth running Hollywood. Some of the top executives today, such as Aaron Spelling and Don Bellisario, are hardly kids. Back in the 1930s, Irving Thalberg was the number-two man under Louis B. Mayer at MGM, the most successful and powerful studio in the world. Thalberg took this position at the age of thirty-one.

However, the young people of today are different from those of the past. They don't want to know the roots of the industry. *Yesterday* is an unspoken word; today is all that matters. Recently two new female agents asked an actor friend of mine to lunch. They had just joined the agency that represented him. They met at the Ivy, a trendy show-biz restaurant. Bill, my friend, was taken aback by their youth and beauty.

"Bill, tell us all about yourself. We want to know everything you've done. What was your first job?"

"Well, after getting out of the service, my first job was *Mister Roberts*."

"Mr. Roberts? Who was he?"

"That was a Broadway play."

"Oh! Who was in it?"

"Henry Fonda was the star."

"Henry Fonda? Oh! Was he any relation to Bridget Fonda?"

I'll guarantee you that Irving Thalberg knew who Sarah Bernhardt was.

Acknowledgments

I would like to express my gratitude to those who contributed their time and knowledge to this book: Gillian Barrett, Rudy Behlmer, Kellie Hagan, Tracy Hall, Kay Henley, Sally Hope, Lynne Kirste, Mimi Melnick, and Anthony Slide.

MARTINIS AND QUAKER OATS WITH BILL FRAWLEY

"*John*, I need you to go to Denver with Bill Frawley," Don Fedderson said.

Frawley had one of the leading roles in Fedderson's popular comedy *My Three Sons*. Following his classic turn as Fred Mertz on *I Love Lucy*, Bill played Uncle Bub on *My Three Sons* for the show's first four-and-a-half seasons. The series starred Fred MacMurray as a widower raising three boys.

During the show's third season, Bill Frawley had to take a trip to Denver, Colorado, for a Quaker Oats convention. Quaker Oats was one of the show's sponsors. This is when the show's executive producer, Don Fedderson, calls to tell me I have to go along because Bill insists. Try to imagine this: We're going to the place where Bill Frawley had been born, a place he hasn't been back to for fifty years. He wants to look up old friends, school chums, and so forth. I'm thinking, good luck finding any of them still alive.

We land at nine in the morning, and Bill insists we stop and have a drink. Nine in the morning! So we have a couple of Bloody Marys. We look for the first three or four people. They've long since passed away. Then Bill wants lunch. He has three martinis with lunch and seems to be fine. (I would have been under the table.) After lunch we try to look up three or four more people; they're also gone. Bill says there's one more guy to look up. We do. We find him in the intensive care unit of a hospital. Bill isn't allowed in to see him. So much for Bill's friends in Denver.

Bill says, "Let's go to my room and have a few drinks and then go to dinner."

He has two Old Fashioneds before dinner in his room, then a couple of scotches at the dinner table, followed by after-dinner drinks. Now here is a man well into his seventies who drinks like a fish. Make that a whale! I'd never seen anything like it before, and I haven't since. Then Bill says he's tired and is going to bed. I remind him that we have to attend the banquet the next evening and that he is expected to speak at five o'clock sharp.

"You'd better get plenty of rest."

"Fine, wake me at nine."

That night I have trouble sleeping because I'm afraid that the next day when I go to get him, well, I don't want to think about it. In the morning I get to his door at five minutes to nine and knock. I hear this raspy old voice: "I said nine! It's not nine. . . . come in, come in!"

I walk in, and the first thing I see is a pitcher of Bloody Marys. I'm thinking, how is he going to make it to the Quaker Oats banquet?

"Call room service and order us some breakfast."

After we eat, Bill tells me he's still thirsty and wants to go down to the bar for a couple of drinks. I try to remind him about the banquet.

"Stop worrying, I'll be there."

We go to the bar, and I lose count of how many drinks he has. All I can think about is getting him to the banquet and in a condition to make a speech. I believe that before, during and after lunch that day, he must have had four or five drinks. I finally get him to his room so he can take a shower and put on a clean suit. While he's in the shower, singing, I call the fellow from Quaker Oats.

"Look, whatever you do, you must have Mr. Frawley be the very first guest speaker, otherwise, I guarantee nothing. Trust me, he's got to be the first speaker."

"I think you're trying to tell me something."

"That's right."

"Well, all these people are here with their wives. They can't wait to meet William Frawley."

"Fine, just make sure he's the first guest speaker!"

We get to the convention. Bill is still walking. The festivities don't start until 6:00 p.m. By that time Bill has had two drinks at the dinner table. A gentleman approaches the dais to speak. Bill has another drink. The guy introduces William Frawley and proceeds to give an intro that lasts at least ten minutes. "He's the greatest this, he's the most wonderful that, everybody loves him, he's America's Uncle Bub," (and on and on). Bill grabs another drink.

Finally, "And now I want to present William Frawley!"

Everybody is standing up and clapping and going crazy to see and hear him. I'm shrinking in my seat, not knowing what is going to happen, but knowing it won't be good. Bill walks up to the microphone and all of these Midwestern couples are standing applauding, leaning forward to get a glimpse of their hero, Uncle Bub of *My Three Sons*. Bill grabs the mike.

"I can only say this. I've seen shit piled before, but never in my life have I seen it piled so high. Good night!"

He walks off. Everybody sits in stunned silence. The Quaker Oats man looks at me indignantly.

"I told you he had to be the first to speak."

On the plane back home, I start dozing and wondering how I ever got into this crazy business.

THANKS FOR THE JOB, DAD!—BARBARA STANWYCK AND GEORGE SANDERS

I got my first job in Hollywood in 1952, reading stories for a possible *Reader's Digest* television series. There were three of us reading stories. We were all interviewed for the job. That was just a formality for me. My father owned the studio called American National.

I remember the other two people I worked with, Joe Stone and Pat Fielder. Joe Stone had been a prizefight referee and wanted to get into the writing end of TV, and Pat Fielder had been a secretary. Pat went on to become a very well-known film and television screenwriter.

The *Reader's Digest* job was simple. Read all of the old *Reader's Digest* magazines and write synopses of the stories that would make good TV shows. I was paid $75 a week. I left the job after ten months. I have never read another *Reader's Digest*. I'm sure it's a wonderful magazine, but I got bored reading the same stories over and over again. The show was turned into a series, and I wound up being fortunate enough to work on it as casting director. Oh yes!—my father still owned the studio.

My father was William Stephens. He had been in the business for years. He was a producer, owner of a production company, and the head of a studio. He produced all of the Dr. Christian movies. He also produced the radio show *Dr. Christian* starring Jean Hersholt. He made a number of B movies—*Jungle Goddess, Thunder in the Pine*—a lot of shows I'm sure you've never heard of. He had been an agent and represented many major motion picture stars, such as Preston Foster and

Joseph Schildkraut (who won an Academy Award for *The Life of Emile Zola*), as well as P. G. Wodehouse, and the director William Dieterle, among others. These are the people I grew up with.

In 1953, shortly after leaving the *Reader's Digest* job, I got my first opportunity to work on a television show as casting director. The show was called *International Police*, which concerned itself with policemen all over the world solving crimes. There was no host; each show featured its own different policeman. *International Police* was a total disaster. The only thing I remember about it is casting Charlie Buchinski in his first leading role. He later became the highest paid motion picture star in the world under the name Charles Bronson.

As a casting director, I remember going to every movie and all the local stage plays I could, trying to acquaint myself with every actor and actress in town. I watched all the TV shows, East Coast as well as West Coast, and got pretty well acquainted with the whole scene.

Due to my father's efforts, I got the chance to cast my first feature, *A Witness to Murder*, in 1954. Chester Erskine produced it, and Roy Rowland directed. It starred Barbara Stanwyck, Gary Merrill, and George Sanders. In the film, Barbara Stanwyck sees Sanders strangle a woman and turns to policeman Merrill for help.

Barbara Stanwyck was one of the nicest ladies I've ever met. I'll never forget our first meeting. She calls me over, introduces herself, and asks me if I've read the script. "Of course I have."

"Did you see the description of my character?"

"Of course." (I wonder what she's getting at.)

"Johnny, in this script I'm a thirty-five-year-old woman. Do you know what that means? I want to be made to look like a thirty-five-year-old woman, which means your job in casting is to make sure that we have an 'elderly' cast surrounding me."

"You got it. Do you want me to tell the assistant director to make sure that the extras around you are all elderly?"

"I've already done that."

I guess the average age of our cast was about eighty-five.

Next I'm introduced to George Sanders.

"Nice to meet you. Never talk to me again. Arrange to have a piano in my dressing room. I play the piano every day. It soothes my nerves. I guess that's it. I'll see you at the end of the show, and if you're on the set, remember, never talk to me."

In those days, agents had to approve their client's contracts. Then the contract had to be signed on the set by the actor along with the W-2 form. I get Sanders's contract. I go down to the set and walk up to his dressing room door. To say I'm a little nervous would be putting it mildly. I timidly knock.

"Yes."

"Hi, it's John Stephens."

"I told you never to bother me."

"Mr. Sanders, you're doing this movie. You want to be paid, don't you? I'll just slip your contract and W-2 under the door for your signature."

The door opens, he grabs the papers, tells me to stay put, signs the papers, and hands them back to me. "That's it?"

"That's it."

Every time the assistant director calls Mr. Sanders to the set, he's right there, knows every line, is absolutely brilliant. He never talks to a single person, not even to Barbara Stanwyck, who would talk to anyone. As soon as a scene is over, he does all his offstage lines and returns to his dressing room.

At the end of the show, Mr. Sanders announces to the entire cast and crew, "I've loved this experience, and as I do on all my shows, I'm giving a party for all of you."

All of a sudden we see the other George Sanders. He plays the piano, has drinks, and couldn't be nicer. He talks with everyone and thanks everyone on the show.

A Witness to Murder wound up being a very good film and to this day it's kind of a cult movie. It was very interesting and very well done with some very good production values. This was my first feature and judging by those that followed, I should have quit while I was ahead!

NEW YORK MOVES WEST—DICKIE WIDMARK AND CHARLES BRONSON

The next TV show I worked on was *Treasury Men in Action*. It was a show out of New York and had very high ratings. The fact that it was scheduled between *Dragnet* and Groucho Marx in *You Bet Your Life* might have helped. In those days if a popular show aired at 8:00 p.m., most people wouldn't change their dial. Remote controls didn't exist. People would stay with the station they were on from 8:00 p.m. to 11:00 p.m. *Treasury Men in Action* was hosted by Walter Greaza, who played the chief in the show's final season. It showed a different Treasury man solving a crime each week. The show aired from 1950 to 1955. I came on board in 1954.

Bob Sloan, the producer, came out from New York with the show. I was assigned to him. Although he was one of the first men I worked with in Hollywood, I remember him to this day. He had a wife and six children. How he had six children, I'll never know—he spent twenty-three out of every twenty-four hours working on his show. He thought of nothing else. Never went to movies, never watched TV, never read the newspaper. His life was *Treasury Men in Action*. He wrote, produced, and edited every episode. He also directed half of them.

We were paying everybody who came in to act on the show $70 a day, which was scale. There were not too many great actors available to us for this salary.

Bob calls me into the office one day. "Johnny, Johnny, I ran into this actor I worked with in New York, and I know he'd love to do our show, so give him a ring."

"Sure, what's his name?"

"He'd love to do our show."

"What's his name, Bob?"

"Dickie Widmark."

"Dickie Widmark? Don't you know what he's been doing?"

"New York radio?"

"Bob, he's been out here a few years since you've seen him. He's one of the biggest stars in Hollywood!"

"He'll do our show, just call him up."

"Fine."

I never called him.

Bob calls me one night after we had cast a show. "Johnny, we have a terrible problem. The actress, Gloria Talbot, who we cast as the soda jerk, lives in Brentwood!"

"So?"

"How could she be working in a malt shop and live in Brentwood?"

"Bob, she's an actress."

We cast an actress who had played a supporting role in *Lost Horizon*, Isabel Jewell. Bob knew who she was (I don't know how) and thought she was going to be perfect. We had her playing an elderly gun moll. At that time, we were working six days a week. We'd rehearse in the loft of American National Studios (the old Eagle-Lion Studios). William Beaudine was the director. He was not at all pleased with the casting of Jewell.

One evening when rehearsal is breaking up, I'm walking back to the rehearsal hall. Nancy Gates, one of the actresses, asks me if I have a date that night. "If you do, you'd better cancel it."

"Why?"

"The rehearsal is over. We're all leaving."

"Yeah."

"Do you notice anyone missing?"

"Isabel?"

"That's right, John, maybe you'd better go up and take a look."

I go up to the loft, and there is Isabel Jewell, dancing and singing, totally nude! After much trouble, I manage to get her dressed and into a taxi. She starts taking her clothes off again. The taxi driver argues about taking her home. I convince him to take her by giving him a large tip. "Just get her home."

We replaced her before the show started.

Things were always crazy on the set of *T-Men in Action*. Once we cast Charlie Buchinski in a lead. Charlie was very unusual. He had had a tough time as a child growing up in the coal mines. Because his family had been so poor, he'd slept in newspapers instead of pajamas. Bob Sloan was directing this particular episode. Charlie comes up to me during rehearsal and in his deep, tough-guy voice says, "I don't like this guy!"

"Give him a chance."

"I said, *I don't like him!*"

I get a phone call from Bob later that day. "Get right down to the set."

"Why?"

"I think Charlie's going to kill me."

I go down to the set. Charlie comes up to me.

"He wants me to put dirt on. I don't want to put dirt on. I lived my whole life in dirt in the coal mines. No more dirt."

We all talked. Charlie put a little dirt on, and we finished the show.

At the end, the show's ratings had slipped. Our time slot was changed. We didn't have the terrific *Dragnet* lead-in any longer.

Bob had an offer to go to 20th Century Fox. He wanted me to go with him. He thought I should get away from my father. The night the last episode of the show finished filming, Bob Sloan went home, wrote out the rerun schedule, mailed it, and went to bed. He had a massive heart attack that night and died. I still think about him.

KATY JURADO NEEDS A JOB
AND TOMMY KIRK GETS HIS START

*T*he next producer I worked with was Jerry Robinson. He produced a show called *The Man Behind the Badge*, which ran from 1953 to 1955. A different person played the man behind the badge every week.

Jerry Robinson never, ever, wanted to meet actors. He didn't like actors, and he didn't like actresses. My job on the show was this: actors and actresses had to have their picture in the *Academy Players Directory*. I had to pick three people for each part from the *Directory*, actors I felt would be right for the part and who would work for $70 a day. Not in book, not considered. God help us if their picture in the *Directory* wasn't what the part called for. Even if I knew the actor could do the part, Jerry would look at the picture and say, "No, no, no, he's not right for a policeman or a gangster. He looks more like a headwaiter."

The actor wouldn't get the part. Actors were chosen solely on their picture in the *Players Directory*. The show lasted one year.

I had an office at American National, the studio my father owned. This little kid used to stand on the corner outside my office. He was kind of cute, about nine or ten years old. I walk outside once and all of a sudden, out of nowhere, this elderly man appears.

"This is my son Tommy, who wants to be an actor. You're a casting director, aren't you?"

"Yes, how did you know?"

"I find out, I find out."

"You want to be an actor, son?"

"Yes sir, I do."

I invite them into my office and give the kid a scene to read, to see how he'll do. He looks the scene over and reads for me. He's brilliant. I tell his father that I think he's really good and that the next time I have any part for a boy his age, I'll definitely bring him in for a reading. His father tells me that Tommy hasn't done anything and doesn't even have an agent. He's hoping I can help him. A part does come up a little later, and I mention Tommy to the director, Johnny Peyser.

"Bring him in."

We bring Tommy in, and he blows us away. He gets the part! We're ready to shoot and Johnny Peyser has an idea. "Let's shoot the rehearsal. We'll tell the crew, but we won't tell Tommy."

Tommy does the scene absolutely brilliantly. Johnny Peyser calls out "Print!" This was the first job that Tommy Kirk ever had. He went on to star in *Spin and Marty* with Tim Considine, *Old Yeller*, *The Shaggy Dog*, and a number of other movies at Disney.

Another show I cast in 1954 was *Quick as a Flash*, a game show hosted by George Jessel. A panel would try to figure out the clues we provided in three-minute segments. The clues were about events, book titles, and so forth. *Quick as a Flash* was more or less a filmed version of the parlor game Charades, except that the actors gave clues through dialogue and costumes.

The producer of *Quick as a Flash* was Richard Lewis. We got along great. Here comes Charlie Buchinski again. I had mentioned him to Dick Lewis. Dick wanted to meet him. Charlie walks in. Charlie had a very, very unusual presence; people were a little bit frightened of him.

"*Hullo.*"

"So Charlie . . ."

"*Yeah.*"

"Nice to meet you."

"*Yeah.*"

"Charlie?"

"*Yeah.*"

"Would you like to read for this part?"

"*You want me to read?!*"

"Well, you don't have to if you don't want to, Charlie."

"*I don't really want to read.*"

"That's okay, Charlie, that's okay."

"Good. That it? Good-bye, thanks Johnny."

Richard Lewis was shocked. "Well, he's got a great face, Johnny, so let's go with him."

We were looking for a lady to do three parts. Earl Kramer, an agent, walks into my office, saying "Johnny, I'm desperate."

"What's the matter, Earl?"

"I've got to get a part for Katy Jurado or she's going to be deported. She's fouled up her visa, and she'll have to go back to Mexico."

I'm stunned. Katy Jurado had been nominated for an Academy Award for her performance in *High Noon* two years before. "Katy Jurado?! Now, Earl, you know we pay $70 a day here. Granted she'd get three parts in three different shows, so it's $210 for the day, but it's only one day's work."

"I'm desperate. I've gone all over. Nobody else has anything for her. I've got to get a part for her in the next couple of days."

"Let me ask the producer."

I go to Richard Lewis's office. "Katy Jurado? You're kidding!"

"No, we can get Katy Jurado for our money."

You know the famous adage, "you get what you pay for"…good luck. We knew nothing about Katy Jurado except that she had been nominated for an Academy Award. We had no idea how she worked. Troublemaker? Hard worker? Unprofessional? Of course I didn't bother to check with any of the people she had worked for. Katy comes to work. The assistant director, Gil Kay, says to me, "I've worked with this woman before. Believe me, it's like pulling teeth."

"Oh come on, it's Katy Jurado."

"Just remember what I told you."

We start filming that morning at eight o'clock. We finish at four o'clock the next morning. It isn't like pulling teeth. It's like a root canal! She can't remember more than two words at a time. She has to run off to her dressing room to get made up again and again. We put it together.

It was a good lesson. When somebody who is very, very big is all of a sudden offered to you at no money, pass.

I did a show in 1955 called *Dear Phoebe* starring Peter Lawford. Lawford played a man who wrote an advice-to-the-lovelorn column for a big city newspaper under the pen name of Phoebe. This was the first time in my young innocent life I was ever exposed to the "politics" of Hollywood: all of the infighting and everything else that goes with it.

Dear Phoebe was created and produced by Alex Gottlieb. Alex was a brilliant and funny man. Peter Lawford was a successful actor who had just come over from his contract at MGM. The director was Don Weis, who had directed Peter in a lot of movies at MGM. The female star of the show, Marcia Henderson, had numerous feature and television credits.

Now what happened was—even as they were filming the pilot, which I didn't do, but heard about—a schism developed and immediately sides were drawn up. It was Peter Lawford and Don Weis against Alex Gottlieb and Marcia Henderson. I'd never been in a situation like this. I would mention an actress to Don. The actress would come on the set, and right away Peter would ask, "Is that Alex's girl?"

"No, Don Weis recommended her."

"Okay, that's good."

Then Alex would come up to me. "Where'd that girl come from, Johnny? Is she one of Don's? I thought so. I don't like her."

The phone calls back and forth. Ten o'clock, eleven o'clock, twelve o'clock at night. The arguments back and forth. How we ever, ever got through that show I'll never know.

On *Dear Phoebe*, character actor Charles Lane played the newspaper publisher. Charlie couldn't remember his own name. The assistant director and prop man would write his lines out and put them in various places on the set unseen by the camera. Charlie would walk around his desk doing his lines. He'd walk over to the typewriter and say three lines. He'd look at the camera, then look down, kind of turn his head, and look right over to where someone would be holding a card up with three more lines. We did every scene that way. You'd see Charlie on screen, and you'd never know that was going on.

That was *Dear Phoebe*. I don't know if anyone ever watched it. It only lasted one year. Was I destined to become the one-year wonder?

THE *GREAT GILDERSLEEVE—UNCHAINED* AND HALL BARTLETT

Another TV show I cast in 1955 was *The Great Gildersleeve*, which had been a radio show. It was about a small town water commissioner. Hal

Peary, who created the character of Gildersleeve for radio, was turned down for the part in the television show by the sponsors, who told him he "just wasn't Gildersleeve." He wasn't the public's perception of Gildersleeve. These were the sponsors. Brilliant men. They cast Willard Waterman, who was more of the country club, snobbish type. Nice man; he just wasn't Gildersleeve. But the sponsors wanted him, so that's who we used.

The Great Gildersleeve was to be directed by Frank Tashlin, a famous movie director. He wrote and directed a lot of funny features at Paramount, such as *Son of Paleface* with Bob Hope and *The Geisha Boy* with Jerry Lewis. Tashlin was married to Mary Costa, an unusual opera singer. Unusual because she was young and attractive. Mary Costa was cast in a minor role in *Gildersleeve*. We had three days to rehearse the pilot and three days to shoot it.

Frank Tashlin comes to me telling me how to make the actors' deals. "I'll rehearse one day with the actors and spend two days prerecording Mary's songs."

"We'll only rehearse the actors one day?"

"That's right, Johnny. I only need them one day." This was strange. We prerecord all of Mary's song numbers. The third day we begin to rehearse with the actors. The rehearsal is scheduled for 9:00 a.m. to 6:00 p.m. At noon we break for lunch. Frank turns to me. "Johnny, let everybody go. We're ready to start filming tomorrow."

"Wow. Okay, Frank."

The network decided not to buy *The Mary Costa Show*.

Also in 1955, I cast a feature, *Unchained*, for Hall Bartlett. Hall was the man who made the movie *Crazylegs* about football player Elroy Hirsch. Hirsch starred in the film. Hall was a nice fellow but had one hang-up as a lot of people in Hollywood do. He was really hung up on athletes. He was completely hung up on Elroy Hirsch, who, while a brilliant football player, was no Marlon Brando.

Hirsch had been fine playing himself in *Crazylegs*. In *Unchained* he played a man who was in prison after having been unjustly accused of committing a crime. Playing a prisoner, without the benefit of stock footage, called for acting. Unfortunately, Elroy was not up to the task.

We were looking for a little kid to play his son. It was a one-day part, one scene only, on location at the Chino minimum-security prison. Hall calls me into his office.

"Johnny, this is absolutely the most important part of the show. It shows what Elroy is really like. He's not a hardened criminal, and we've got to see the real love between a father and his son. I need the best kid actor we can get. I hear you're good with kid actors. Who would you suggest?"

"What's the budget?"

"The budget is whatever we have to pay."

"Well, the only kid I know who'd be perfect is Tim Considine. He starred in the remake of *The Champ* with Red Skelton."

"I saw that movie; he was great. Get him."

"Well, now, I don't know if he'll do a one-day part. He's done a lot of big things at Metro; he's left MGM and is up for a contract at Disney."

"Get him!"

I call Tim directly. He says he'll do it for me. Then I call his agent, Sam Armstrong, and he says the same thing. When I get Tim, Hall Bartlett thinks I'm the all-time great casting director. Tim comes in and does the part. He's very good. After the filming, the agents in town, as is their wont, ask Hall how much he paid Tim.

"We got him for $1,000."

"$1,000?! And John Stephens is your casting director, right?"

"Right, he cast the show."

"Don't you know that he and Tim go way back? John is very friendly with his whole family. You could have gotten him for $300."

Hall Bartlett never spoke to me again!

Next I had the good fortune to work for one of the most intelligent men I've ever known in the industry, Howard Koch.

I RUIN A PREVIEW

I learned more from Howard Koch than I have from anyone before or since. He and his partner, Aubrey Schenck, had a company called Schenck & Koch. I worked for them from 1955 through 1956. They used different production names. Bel Air Productions was the main one. Schenck & Koch made six-day features using the same directors, the same actors, and the same story over and over again. All they did was switch locales. They had a fellow in business with them who was a distributor from United Artists. He would make sure all of their movies were in theaters. Sometimes instead of six-day movies, we'd go on location and make two movies in eleven days. As I said, we had *one* story. There was the hero. There was the heroine. In the beginning the hero and the heroine did not like each other. That was a given. The heroine had a father. He was an elderly man, a scientist, an archeologist, or a chemist. They'd be going to Egypt to dig for artifacts or to Greece to discover a secret formula or to some sea to look for a sea monster. There were two funny guys, like Abbott and Costello, always making jokes and screwing up. There was the bad guy. Always the same guy. He had his eye out for the heroine. Then there was the bad girl who always had her eye on the hero. That was the story. We did this over and over and over. I'm sure that without seeing these movies, and I doubt that you did, you can guess the outcome. Because the characters trekked from one place to another to fulfill their mission, these films were called trek shows.

Howard Koch could get any location he wanted. He was the greatest talker and the greatest thinker I've ever known. Aubrey Schenck would go to the locations Howard had gotten, and we'd lose them all because of Aubrey's manners and his innate ability to antagonize anyone and everyone. Then Howard would return, and we'd get all the locations back.

Howard never wanted to waste time in production. The crew would fly up to Kanab, Utah, his favorite place to film. The first location in Kanab would be ten minutes from the airport. The production company would be off the plane and shooting in thirty minutes. Companies today go to the hotel, check in, get on a bus, leave for location, and usually get a half a page of script shot the first day. Howard's companies got six or seven pages on the first location day.

There were a lot of great people working for Schenck & Koch. They had a production manager, Hal Klein, whom I had the good fortune to learn a lot from and years later was able to hire on the TV series *How the West Was Won*. The thing about Howard's way of doing things was the crews ran the shows. The actors didn't. That's the way it was.

Funny things would happen at Schenck & Koch. My phone rings one day. It's Aubrey. "Come in here, kid, come in here. You know we're previewing *The Pharaoh's Curse* tonight. Are you going to be there?"

"Yes."

"Do you know where it is?"

"No."

"It's at the Fox Beverly Theater."

"In Beverly Hills?"

"Yes, isn't that great?"

I think he's kidding. In those days the marquee of the Fox Beverly would read MAJOR STUDIO PREVIEW TONIGHT, and he's talking about a Friday night in Beverly Hills, where the people would be expecting to see something with Marlon Brando or Clark Gable at the very least.

Aubrey continues, "Here's what I want you to do. Get three girls. We'll pay them to get into the theater. Remember the movie with Ray Milland, *The Uninvited?*"

"Yeah."

"Remember when the door slammed and everyone in the audience was so shocked they screamed?"

"Yeah."

"Now here's the script. See right here where the mummy appears?"

"Yeah."

"I want you to have those girls scream, and the audience will go hysterical. This movie will be a big success. It will be colossal."

I'm still waiting for the joke that never comes. He's serious. Now I've got to go and find three girls to waste their Friday night for nothing, to sit in the Fox Beverly Theater, and scream. I finally find this girl who I know from college, Maxine Griffith, who says she'll do it and can bring a couple of friends. "By the way, Maxine, guess what? You won't have to pay your way in."

I meet the girls outside the theater, show them the script, make certain that they understand what they're supposed to do, and give them money for their tickets. I go into the theater. It's packed with these Beverly Hills people anxiously waiting to see a film with . . . Clark Gable? Spencer Tracy? Who's it gonna be?

The lights go out, the curtain parts. Up on the screen comes "A Bel Air Production." There's a little bit of tittering in the audience. Then comes "Schenck & Koch" and the audience laughs out loud. As each credit appears, there's more and more laughter. Then comes the booing, hissing, and foot stamping. The audience goes absolutely berserk! Where's

Brando? Where's Gable? Who's Marla English? As the movie progresses, everything that is supposed to be horrifying becomes funny. There isn't a single thing the audience doesn't laugh at. This is supposed to be a horror film, and everyone is reacting as if it were a comedy. Of course, it's so bad that it *is* a comedy.

Now comes the moment when the girls are supposed to scream. It happens that there's a pause in the laughter just before the girls begin screaming. Instead of gasps of shock, the audience erupts into gales of laughter. It's a total disaster.

By the time the film ends, I don't think there are more than twenty people in the audience, and that's counting the crew, the three girls, and myself. Then the corker. As I'm leaving, Aubrey comes up and chews me out.

"You should have used your head. Once you saw the way the audience was reacting, you should have stopped those girls. They ruined the whole movie." Right, a great movie ruined!

"WHY DID YOU BRING THAT BUM IN HERE?"

I got to work on two good movies at Schenck & Koch. One was *Shield for Murder* with Edmund O'Brien, who is one of the greatest actors I ever worked with. He could do anything, from Shakespeare to a lowly Bowery bum. He won an Academy Award for his role in *The Barefoot Contessa*. The other good movie was *Big House USA*. Howard Koch got permission to film in the maximum-security area of the Canon City Prison in Canon City, Colorado. Ralph Meeker was cast. He had just lost the lead in *Picnic*—a part he had created on Broadway—to William Holden. You can imagine his frame of mind, going from losing *Picnic* to winding up in *Big House USA* for Schenck & Koch.

We also had Charlie Buchinski, who was now going by the name Bronson and whose star was on the rise; Broderick Crawford from TV's *Highway Patrol* and an Academy Award winner for *All the King's Men*; Lon Chaney Jr., the star of *The Wolf Man* and other horror films; and Bill Tallman, who became famous as the district attorney in the *Perry Mason* television series. The entire cast and crew, with the exception of Charlie Bronson, Ralph Meeker, and myself, were drunk the whole time. Lon Chaney Jr. was the only man I ever met who was drunk twenty-four hours a day. Bill Tallman was a mean drunk. Brod Crawford was a happy drunk. He was the only happy person on the location. Ralph Meeker was usually mad. Charlie was always mad. When our actors walked through the maximum-security area of the Canon City Prison, the prisoners were scared.

Schenck & Koch did a lot of Westerns. All of the actors had to do their own stunts. We used two professional stuntmen, Red Morgan and Al Wyatt. Red and Al did the main stunts, but otherwise the actors had to do their own. Everybody had to do their own riding. At interviews, I'd ask the actors if they could ride.

"Do I ride? Why, I was raised on a ranch."

They wouldn't tell me it was an avocado ranch! When they'd get up to the location, the director, Les Selander, would find a guy who he knew didn't ride. He'd have the actor mount a horse, slap the horse on the rear, and off the horse would go. And off the rider would go!

Sometimes, like in *Big House USA*, Schenck and Koch wanted to cast against type. I remembered seeing *Riot in Cell Block Eleven* with a very unusual actor playing the prison warden. A real rough, tough-looking guy, Emile Meyer, who spoke with a lisp. He was excellent. I also remembered Meyer's performance as Ryker, the lead heavy in the movie *Shane*. I bring him in to meet Schenck and Koch. They're thrilled. Going through the dailies for *Big House*, Meyer seems to be great. After production on *Big House* finishes, and we're starting to cast for the next film, Aubrey calls me in.

"Ya know whatcha gotta do, kid. Ya gotta bring us some more people like Emile Meyer. When we suggested Emile Meyer to you, you didn't know who was he was . . . you gotta start thinking like that. Bring us more Emile Meyers."

"Right, Aubrey."

Out comes *Big House USA*. The reviews are quite good. The only person the critics rap is Emile Meyer. "A good movie that couldn't be ruined by the amateurish Emile Meyer." Aubrey calls me in again.

"Don't bring us any more bums like Emile Meyer. Use your head."

"Right, Aubrey, never again."

Every time we'd start a new show, Aubrey would call me into his office. "Johnny, Johnny, what we want are some new faces."

I would obey orders and bring in new faces. Here is the way the casting sessions went. Let's say I brought in a new person, "Jim Adams," for Part D, a small three-line part. Jim Adams would give a reading before Aubrey and Howard. They'd tell him it was a great reading and then tell me, with Jim in the room, that maybe he would be better for Part C because United Artists is looking for new faces and it's a bigger part. Aubrey would turn to Jim Adams and explain that Part C would be better for him because that character runs through the entire film and would give him a chance to show his range of emotions. At this point, Jim Adams would get very excited at the prospect of getting the bigger part. Then Howard would chime in, "You know, I know Jim's work, and he's great, so what about Part B, the heavy? You know, Jim, this part could do for you what *From Here to Eternity* did for Sinatra."

Then Aubrey would come up with the topper. "You know, Howard, new faces, new faces . . . why can't Jim play the lead? I know United Artists will back us one hundred percent."

By now Jim Adams would be in seventh heaven listening to this.

Aubrey would always close with these words: "You know, Johnny, you ought to use your head. Think about these people not as actors doing small parts but think of the possibilities and ranges these people have; think about making people stars. That's why you're here; we want you to think that way. You know, Jim, I think Johnny brought you in for the wrong part, and we're going to push for you definitely for the lead. The worst you'll get is Part B. Do you agree with me, Howard?"

"Absolutely, absolutely."

"Thanks for coming in, Jim! And Johnny, you've gotta think this way and stop bringing in these people and insulting them like this."

The door would shut. Aubrey would turn to me. "Why did you bring that bum in here?"

By the time the show started filming, Jim's agent would run into Howard on the lot. The agent would ask what had happened. "Why isn't Jim Adams in the show, when he was told he'd probably get the lead or at least the role of the heavy? He wasn't even called back to do the part that John Stephens brought him in to read for."

"Oh no, someone slipped up, you'd better get ahold of Johnny and tell him I'm really mad about this."

The agent would call. I'd take the call and time after time would say, as per orders, "I screwed up. I'm sorry. What can I do? I'm casting a number of other shows, I'll find something else for him, I promise you."

At last, after a year and a half of the same story, I snapped. When an agent called I finally told him, "Look, Aubrey Schenck said your client's a bum."

That afternoon I was looking for another job.

AARON SPELLING, CHUCK CONNORS, AND ANGIE DICKINSON

My father and I left to go to his independent company, Conne-Stephens Productions. His partner was Ed Conne. What a perfect name. They were going to do four pilots. I was assigned to produce two of them. In those days when you did a pilot, you got money from backers who owned fifty percent of the profits of the show.

The first show I decided to do was a Western. I wanted Aaron Spelling to write the pilot script. He was not a writer but a $70-a-day actor. I met him through his wife, Carolyn Jones, an up-and-coming actress. Carolyn and Aaron convinced me that Aaron had a lot of writing talent and that he was also a big Western buff.

Aaron came up with an idea for a show, *Big Foot Wallace*. It was about a real-life Western hero who was a gun for hire, but always on the side of the law. Aaron had a writing partner, Paul Richards. Paul was also an actor. Aaron and Paul had been writing together for some time but had never sold anything. I told my father I wanted them. "Whomever you want is fine. They'd better turn in a good script."

Leslie Martinson was hired as the director. In looking for the right actor for the lead, I came up with Chuck Connors. He played baseball for the old Los Angeles Angels of the Pacific Coast League. His acting had been limited to small roles. We signed Chuck, and we were off and running with my first show as a producer.

You always want to start any kind of action-adventure show with a great one-day player who explains the setup to the hero. I learned this from Schenck & Koch. The actor would set up the back story and tell the hero and the rest of the cast what was expected of them and how difficult their job would be. The one actor I'd worked with a lot and thought would really be great for this part was Emory Parnell. Emory came in to do his seven-page scene. This was to take up the morning. As luck would have it, it took the entire day. Emory couldn't remember his own name let alone anyone else's. I call his agent late that night to tell him about it.

"John, this can happen with day players, stars, anybody. Sometimes terrible things happen in their personal lives. In Emory's case, it happened last night. After twenty-five years of marriage, his wife left him." That did not get us off to a very good start.

We finished the pilot. It was under the auspices of the William Morris Agency. We came close to selling the pilot a number of times, but it just never quite worked out. We decided that maybe it didn't sell because we didn't show Chuck Connors off in the right light. Aaron Spelling came up with a new idea for the end of *Big Foot Wallace*—put Chuck in a Western goods store. Have him walking around, spinning some yarns about the Old West. I suggested we bring his children in. We did this and shot about a half-day's footage. The revised pilot looked even better, but still no sale.

At this time, Carolyn Jones, Aaron Spelling's wife, was becoming a big star. The William Morris Agency wooed her away from her smaller agent with the promise of bigger and better parts. She made the decision to go with them, but under the stipulation that they take Aaron on as a client. She pushed them to look at *Big Foot Wallace* again, so they would see they were getting a wonderful writer. The William Morris people viewed it again (remember, they were selling the show), and the part that really interested them was Chuck Connors telling Old West stories. Aaron was called into the office and offered a deal to write for the *Zane Grey Theater* television series starring Dick Powell. Powell had seen *Big Foot* and loved Aaron's opening. Aaron began to write the openings and closings for *Zane Grey Theater* and, as we all know, went on to become one of the most prominent producers in the history of Hollywood television.

The second pilot I did for my father was called *Arabian Nights*. Actor Rex Ingram—he of the great voice and presence—would narrate fictitious stories. John Barrymore Jr. was our star. We needed a child actor to play opposite John. I called the agent of the young boy I mentioned earlier, Tommy Kirk.

"You gave him his start. He'll definitely do it for you."

Barrymore was married to Cara Williams, a well-known character actress and lady about town. Cara was not only his wife, but also his business manager, agent, nursemaid, and bodyguard. She told me in the interview before we set the deal with John that he would be difficult. "The only way to be taken seriously in Hollywood, and to become a star, is to be difficult." Believe me, John lived up to being difficult and then some.

We start rehearsing, and we have to check with Station 12 at the Screen Actors Guild to make sure all the actors' dues have been paid and that they are in good standing with the Guild. When I call Station 12, I'm told that John Barrymore Jr. owes $1,500 in back dues. I go to Cara and explain that we can't do anything until John's dues are paid. She assures me that she'll have a check to us that afternoon.

This is a pilot and we have the luxury of rehearsing for three days before starting to film. At the end of the third day of rehearsal, the dues still haven't been paid. I take a chance.

"Cara, we're going to replace John. We're starting to film tomorrow. John can't work, and I'm bringing in another actor to replace him."

"Bullshit!"

Miraculously the check appeared that afternoon.

Arabian Nights was a show that had good intentions, but failed. The William Morris Agency, which represented Conne-Stephens, looked at it and said they would not even attempt to sell the show. I couldn't blame them.

As we were wrapping postproduction, I got a call from a director whom I had worked with on *The Man Behind the Badge*, Gerald Mayer. At that time Gerald was directing a show called *The Millionaire* for Don Fedderson Productions. They needed an actress for the leading role in an upcoming episode and wanted a new face. The character was a chorus girl. He asked if I knew anyone who could play the part. I told him about Angie Dickinson, a young actress I had worked with a few times. "Call her agent, Sam Armstrong."

It was the first starring role that Angie ever had on television.

Soon afterward, I received a call from Fred Henry, also of Don Fedderson Productions. Fred thanked me for recommending Angie. He said we should get together some time and discuss a possible job. I figured that after going from casting director for my father to producer for my father, maybe I was ready to go out and see what the real world was like.

ENCOUNTERS WITH BETTY WHITE
AND TALLULAH BANKHEAD

I go in to meet with Fred Henry. My interview lasts an hour or so. We get along great.

"I'd like to hire you. Your starting salary will be $150 a week. You'll have to meet with Don Fedderson. He has something in mind for you."

I go in to meet with Don Fedderson, whose offices are on El Camino Drive in Beverly Hills. I sit in the outer office with Lil Holmes, his secretary of many years.

"Would you like to read the trades, Mr. Stephens?"

"Thank you very much."

I pick up *Variety*. The headline reads "Liberace Does Huge Business at Hollywood Bowl."

"Liberace! Can you believe that?!"

Miss Holmes comes to my rescue.

"Isn't he wonderful? Isn't Liberace just great? You know that Mr. Fedderson handles him. He produces all of his shows."

To which I immediately reply, "Yes, he's sensational!" (Saved by the bell.)

Don Fedderson calls me into his office.

"Fred likes you, and I want you to start right away on a show called *The Miracle*. Your job will be to go around the country gathering stories on different miracles. Put them into story form. Then we'll do a pilot script and you'll produce the pilot."

This sounded great. I started working for Don Fedderson on July 11, 1956. I spent the next few months traveling all over the country, gathering material for *The Miracle*. That show never went to pilot, but I stayed at Fedderson Productions, working on television series, pilots, and even commercials, until April 1971.

Two weeks after I return from my travels, Don Fedderson calls me into the office for a meeting with George Tibbles and Betty White. I'd never heard of either of them. It turns out the meeting is about having sold the show *Date with the Angels.* Everyone is excited.

The offices will be located at Desilu Studios on Cahuenga Boulevard in Hollywood. Betty White is the star of the show, and Bill Williams is her costar. They'll play the Angels, a young married couple going through various trials and tribulations. George Tibbles is the writer-producer, and Don Fedderson is the executive producer. I sit and listen to them discuss various aspects of the show. I begin to wonder what I'm doing here.

Betty and George are very cordial. Betty asks, "What will John be doing?"

"John will be in charge of everything."

I'm thinking, what does that mean? I've never really been "in charge" of anything. I have no idea what to expect.

The meeting breaks up with everyone agreeing to start getting the offices set up. We'd meet again in a week or so, and get things going. I run up to Fred Henry's office and tell him about the meeting. He already knows about it.

"What am I in charge of?"

"Just keep your mouth shut and learn."

"Can't I ever talk?"

"Yes, when someone says to talk, talk. Just make sure everything runs smoothly."

I must admit that when I went home, I spent a sleepless night. How could I possibly make a go of this? It sounded like a production manager's job. I didn't know anything about production managing. I'd always been on the creative end of things. I'd produced, helped to write, and done casting. All of a sudden I'm a production manager?

We got our offices set up at Desilu Cahuenga. We started casting. We had a sensational supporting cast: Maudie Prickett, Richard Deacon, Burt Mustin, and Richard Reeves. Smiling Jack Smith sang the theme song.

After we finished casting, I had to hire the crew. I really didn't hire them; I had to approve them. Jim Paisley was the assistant production manager at Desilu. He was to bring in crew people to meet with my approval.

I'll never forget the first man he brought into my office right after lunch. His face is as red as a beet and to say he's drunk would be putting it mildly. Jim Paisley says, "This is your first assistant director, Sid Sidman."

I'm thinking to myself, do I have any choice in this? But obviously I don't. "Fine, nice to meet you, Sid."

He mumbles a few words and walks out. Jim turns to me. "John, you're going to love Sid."

About an hour later Jim returns to my office with a property man, Carl Nugent. It was almost the same situation; Carl wasn't quite as inebriated as Sid but definitely full of the sauce. Most of the crew members that come in are like this. I can see that this is really going to be some crew.

What I didn't know then is that back in the late 1950s, many people had a drinking "opportunity" when they were not filming. Sid and Carl were the best I ever worked with, period. In fact, the whole crew that Jim gave me was sensational.

Things looked bright. Our show was scheduled to follow Frank Sinatra's. Sinatra was coming back to TV after his hit film, *From Here to Eternity*. His show was going to be on at 9:00 p.m. Thursday nights on ABC. We followed at 9:30 p.m. We figured Sinatra would be in the top ten and so would *Date with the Angels*. To cut to the chase, Sinatra wasn't even in the top forty. *Date with the Angels* wasn't even in the top seventy. However, we were contracted to do twenty-six episodes.

Don calls me into his office. "You know the show isn't doing as well as it should be. We are going to go out on a twenty-six city tour with Betty and let the audience get to know Betty White."

This was called a "big city Nielsen tour." Actors don't do this anymore. Now they go on TV talk shows to plug whatever series they're doing. In the old days, actors had to go on tour, be interviewed by the press, and appear on local radio and TV talk shows. Don says he's talked to Betty and that she would like me to go with her.

"No."

Don doesn't ask me why, but I volunteer the reason. "I don't think I could help her; I'm very shy in those situations."

"Okay."

That's the way that company operated. If you were told to do something, you did it. But if you were asked to do something, you had your choice, and no one ever questioned you. I explained it to Betty. She understood.

Betty White had the most amazing memory of anyone I ever worked with. I found out her secret. We would bring someone in for casting. She would insist on all my notes after casting and then give the notes to her mother, Tess, who kept a complete file on everybody Betty ever met or worked with. If the person ever came in again, she would always know them and put them at ease. It wasn't just Tess's work, it was Betty's unbelievable memory. We did a Christmas show once and decided to use the children of the crew members as extras. We rehearsed for three days. In three days, Betty knew the name of every single crew member's child. There were thirty children! She committed every one of them to memory and introduced them to the audience before the show began.

One week, Don informs me that his best friend, Danny Thomas, will be doing next week's show. We're all excited about that, as Danny is a giant name, funny, and appealing to our audience. The Desilu stage where we shot seated 300 people. To get 300 people, I had 2,000 tickets printed up each week. I circulated them everywhere.

On Tuesday Danny Thomas is sent the script. I find out late Tuesday afternoon that Danny has called Don to tell him he can't do the show. It was supposed to be one scene, but the part has been expanded to the extent that he's in every scene. "I can't do this, I've got my own show to do."

Don pleads with him, but Danny won't budge. There we are—two days from filming and no star. Don has a brilliant idea.

"Let's do an All-Star show! We'll give the stars $70 a day, a color TV, and let them plug any album, TV show, or movie they have coming up. I'll get Liberace, and I know I can get Hugh O'Brien because he has a Western album coming out. Johnny, I hear Tallulah Bankhead is finishing a guest shot on *I Love Lucy*. She'd do our show. Go see her and make her the offer. Just tell her it's *Date with the Angels* with Betty White. Johnny, make sure you get her."

I'd never met Tallulah but had certainly heard about her. I knew the assistant director on *I Love Lucy*, Ed Hillie. I go to see Ed on the *Lucy* stage. I tell him I need to talk to Tallulah Bankhead. He asks me why. I explain and he gives me a strange look. "Well, it's your life, not mine. She's in that dressing room right over there."

I walk over to her dressing room and knock on the door. This loud voice calls out, "Whoever the hell it is, come in!"

I walk in and close the door.

"Who are you?"

"I'm John Stephens with the *Date with the Angels* show."

"With what show?"

"It's a show with Betty White"

"Who the fuck is Betty White?"

I turn and quickly leave. I go back to Don Fedderson's office. "Miss Bankhead says she'd love to do the show, but she's not available."

KEENAN WYNN, THE ACTOR AND THE WRITER

$\mathcal{A}$fter twenty-six episodes, *Date with the Angels* was cancelled. However, the gentleman in charge of Plymouth advertising at the time, Jack Minor, happened to be Don Fedderson's brother-in-law. Jack convinced Plymouth to pick us up for thirteen more episodes. The new show would be called *The Betty White Show*, a variety show, and would begin airing in 1957. The show would be done live, and the production would be moved over to ABC Studios. Don and Fred call me into the office.

"We have thirteen more shows to do. This is exactly how much you have to spend, don't go a dime over it; you can even go a dime under it! We know the show is going to be gone, they've already told us that. We're going to save all the money we can. We're going to get guest stars because MCA [the group with which Don Fedderson was aligned and that actually sold the show] has agreed to use all of their people who owe them favors as our guest stars. By the way, don't bother to call us, we'll call you. We'll be down for rehearsals and filming. Otherwise, do it all. We trust you."

Naturally some of the decisions that I have to make during the ensuing thirteen weeks do not go down too well with Betty or George Tibbles. For instance, there was this very good choreographer, Jack Baker. I call him in once to do some choreography on a show where we need dancers. The only thing is, the dancers also have to sing. Well, the singers cost more money, but the dancers don't sing. Jack is confused.

"Well, you'll have singers doing the singing, right?"

"No, we'll have the dancers doing the singing."

"They can't sing."

"It'll sound okay, have them sing."

Poor Jimmy Kern, the director. When we shot at Desilu, there would be about two hours between dress rehearsal and the actual show. He'd go to Lucey's Bar and Grill down the street, and come back a wee bit under the weather. During the live show, he'd come back a lot under the weather! Jimmy was the only carryover to the live show except Betty and George. I was "Jack of all trades, master of none."

We have Cornell Wilde as a guest star. I call him. "Let me give you the rehearsal schedule—"

"Oh no, let me give *you my* rehearsal schedule, which had better fit in with your rehearsal schedule, or I won't be there!"

He gives me his schedule, which obviously becomes our schedule. We get through with guest stars such as Basil Rathbone, Peter Lorre, and Boris Karloff—and their schedules. On this show I didn't even have to make out schedules. What you have to learn in TV is a saying I often use, one that Fred De Cordova taught me: "In television, there are no problems, only opportunities." After all, we weren't curing a major disease. Whatever happened was going to happen, one way or the other.

Keenan Wynn was one our guest stars. After the first reading, Keenan says, "This is shit! I can't do this."

We tell him that he's committed.

"Okay, I'll rewrite it over the weekend. I still think it's shit."

He comes back on Monday with his rewrite. It's worse than the original. On Thursday, we're in the dress rehearsal, a few hours away from the live show. We finish the rehearsal. Keenan turns to me and says, "This is really shit!"

"You wrote it."

"I don't care, it's awful, it's terrible, and I'm not going to do it."

"Keenan, this is a live show. If you don't do it, we have no show."

"You have no show anyway!"

I call his agent, Bill Robinson. "You'd better come over here because we're in deep trouble, to put it mildly."

Bill comes over, and we have a long talk. Then he and Keenan go into a dressing room. I can't hear what's being said, but there's a lot of yelling and screaming. Finally Bill Robinson comes out.

"John, he'll do the show, but I don't recommend you ever call him again."

Fate plays strange tricks. My wife, actress Joan Vohs, did a pilot starring Bob Mathis and Keenan Wynn called *The Trouble Shooters.* Robert Altman directed. Of course Keenan loved Joan. Four weeks later Joan and I are in the Golden Bull steak house in Santa Monica. Who walks in but Keenan! I can't hide. He greets Joan, then looks at me. I slowly try to sink under the table. "I know you."

"No, I don't think so."

"I never forget a face."

"We've never met; I have a very common face."

"Really, you seem very familiar."

Keenan shakes his head and walks away, not convinced. I turn to Joan. "Let's get out of here."

Unfortunately, I never worked with Betty White again, but I did see her from time to time. She is a beautiful lady and eventually got the acclaim she so richly deserved.

The next show I was called upon to do was *The Millionaire*. It was going into its sixth season and was a huge success.

GOOD DAYS AND BAD NIGHTS ON *THE MILLIONAIRE*

The Millionaire was probably the most fun show I ever worked on. New stories every week, with different actors and directors. In each episode a character named Michael Anthony, played by Marvin Miller, handed a deserving recipient a tax-free check for one million dollars. The money came from a billionaire, John Beresford Tipton, voiced by Paul Frees. Each story showed how the money changed the lives of the people who received it, always for the better. Many members of our audience believed that these were true stories, and we received as many as five hundred letters a week from people asking to be considered as recipients of the million dollars.

The Millionaire went on the air in 1954, and ran for seven years. It was very popular. I worked on the show for its final two years.

Paul Frees received $70 per episode for his work. He came down from San Francisco at his convenience. We paid his plane fare, and he usually did five episodes in one day. It was a lot of fun shooting the openings. The audience couldn't see Paul. They'd only hear his offstage voice.

We could shoot the openings anywhere because the Tipton estate was supposedly so humongous that anywhere could be a part of the estate.

Don Fedderson dealt with actors who became problems in one of three ways. Their characters were sent away on a long journey never to return, they got married and left town, or they died unexpectedly. It was their choice. No one ever got the best of Don Fedderson. I learned a lot from the way he operated.

We had a lot of guest stars on the show. The top salary for the guest stars was $1,000. If an actor or actress came in from out of town, they'd also receive round-trip transportation and accommodation at the Chateau Marmont. I was fortunate enough to work with my wife Joan on an episode entitled "Lights Out." We brought Dick York out from New York to costar. On the episode I made a great friend in Dick York. But as you'll see, friendship is fleeting, especially in show biz!

My most difficult job on *The Millionaire* was to find a part in every episode for Tido Fedderson, Don's wife. Some episodes only had two or three characters. In the episode "Lights Out," my wife and Dick York played a couple who had no money. There were only two other people in the cast. I had to think quickly. I made Tido play the role of Joan's dressmaker.

We do a scene in Joan's small apartment and Tido is taking Joan's measurements. Don sees the dailies, a screening of an assemblage of all the developed film from the prior day's work. "How could these people who have no money possibly afford a dressmaker?" I had no answer.

On another episode, Tido was to play a nun. She calls me the night before. "I'm playing a nun tomorrow?"

"Yes, Tido."

"Okay, I can do that. John, do nuns ever wear fur coats?"

"No, Tido, they don't."

"Well, can I just—"

"No, Tido, you can't wear a fur coat!"

"All right."

The next morning Tido comes to the studio in full makeup. The makeup department has to spend an hour removing the makeup so she'll look like a nun. On the lunch break, she has someone pour her a cocktail, and she drives off in her convertible, with the top down, to the Vine Street Brown Derby for lunch with the cocktail in the cocktail holder. (In those days many cars had cocktail holders.) What a sight—a nun driving a convertible with the top down, drinking a whiskey sour!

The next year an episode was coming up for which we didn't have a completed script. Milton Merlin, writer and story editor, and Fred Henry were discussing it with me. Fred asks, "Isn't Dick York a friend of yours?

"Well, not exactly a friend, we did one show together and got along great."

"Why don't you talk him into doing the show? We'll have the script out no later than tomorrow, but we need to get his okay now. The script is going to be good. Right, Milton?"

"Absolutely, Fred."

"Okay, I'll take your word for it."

I call Dick's agent, who says he'll check with Dick and get back to me. Dick calls me up a couple hours later.

"John, I'll do it for you. Normally I wouldn't commit to a show without seeing the script, but if you say it's good, I'll trust your judgment. I'll definitely do it."

"Great. I'll even pick you up at the airport. Dick, tell you what. Why don't you stay with Joan and me, as we have plenty of room."

"Is Joan going to be in the show with me?"

"No, we're having our first baby. She can't work."

"Congratulations! Tell her I'm looking forward to seeing her. I'll see you at the airport."

"Great."

The next day I get the script. It's the day before I'm to pick up Dick. I read the script. I'm stunned. It's absolutely dreadful. Here I am, committed to an actor whom I've assured the script will be great. Not only am I picking him up at the airport, but he'll be staying with Joan and me during the filming.

I go to Milton and ask if the script is going to change. "Oh sure, wait until rehearsal. What do you think Dick will say when he reads it?"

I don't answer.

I tell Fred Henry about the situation. He laughs. "It'll all work it out, don't worry."

The next day I pick Dick up. He's in a great mood. I drive him home, and Joan greets us. There's small talk, and I offer Dick a cocktail.

He says, "Why don't you give me the script, and I'll take my drink into my room and read it before dinner."

He goes off with the script and his drink. I turn to Joan. "Do you think I should take him in a few more drinks while he's reading the script?"

Forty-five minutes later Dick comes out. He doesn't say a word. Through dinner he makes a little polite chatter, a little more polite chatter after dinner, then he excuses himself and goes to bed.

The next morning is Saturday. I ask Dick if I can take him around town to see some of the sights.

"No thanks. I'll just stay in my room and read." I hope he's not going to read the script again.

On Sunday Joan and I drop Dick off at Mass. We go to our church and pick him up afterwards. We all go to breakfast. There's polite, but restrained, chatter the rest of the day. After dinner Dick goes to bed.

The next day we're off to rehearsal. While driving in to the studio, Dick asks me if the script will change. "I'm sure it will."

"John, it had certainly better."

Believe me, Dick York is one of the nicest guys in the world. Most actors would have just gotten up and gone back to New York. The ensuing week is one of the worst weeks of my life. Thank goodness it's only a two-day show. The script doesn't get any worse, but it doesn't get any better! Dick does the show. He never speaks to me at night. He only talks to Joan about the upcoming birth. Finally it's over.

"John, you've been nice to me, and I appreciate it. Good luck, God bless you, Joan, and the child. I'll get myself to the airport."

While doing a pilot some years later, Milton Merlin comes to me.

"John, Dick York is a good friend of yours. He'd be perfect for the lead in this pilot we're doing. Call him up."

I never made that call.

I made another mistake after watching a live show out of New York, *Winterset.* I was watching the show with my wife. I kept dozing off. At one point, I asked Joan, "Will you please get the name of that old man? He's sensational. He has an interesting look."

His name was Anatol Winagrodoff. A few months later an agent, Rikki Barr, walks into my office. In going through her book, I see a photo of Winagrodoff. "Rikki, you handle Anatol Winagrodoff?"

"Yes, did you see him in *Winterset*? Wasn't he great?"

"Yeah, he was great."

"Guess what, John, he happens to be in town."

"No kidding, would he do a *Millionaire* for $150 a day? It's only a one-day part."

"He'd love to."

"Without reading the script first?"

"Of course, he'd love to do it."

I go into Fred Henry's office and tell him I can get this guy to play Mona Freeman's law clerk. (Mona was the guest star that week.) I tell Fred about having seen Anatol in *Winterset* and then tell Jimmy Sheldon, the director, about him. Neither had seen *Winterset*, but both of them say if I'm so excited about this guy, it's fine with them. Hire him.

In those days, it was the Screen Actors Guild's policy to have day players sign their contracts in the production office. It's the first day of rehearsal; I'm sitting in my office. I hear someone mumbling in the outer office. Betty Jane Metz, Fred Henry's secretary, calls to me that someone is out there to see me. She can't understand a word he's saying.

I go out to see who it is. It's Anatol Winagrodoff. He mumbles something to me. I can't understand him either. I discover he's Russian and can barely speak a word of English. I'm shell-shocked! I take him down to the set and introduce him to the director. Jimmy Sheldon is speechless.

"Jimmy, I've got to get back to the office."

"No, John, I want you here for rehearsal. Send Mr. Winagrodoff to makeup and wardrobe. And John, you stay right here."

I'll never forget the first line Mr. Winagrodoff delivers in rehearsal: "Here are the affidavits you wanted prepared." No one could understand a single word. Mona Freeman, reading her script with her glasses on, stops cold, takes her glasses off and stares at me in amazement. Jimmy just looks at me. "Thanks a lot, John."

I slink off the set, go straight into Fred Henry's office, and tell him what's happened. As bad as it is, and it's terrible, I guess I make it sound even worse. Fred tries to calm me down. "I'd better not tell Don. Let's just wait until dailies."

The dailies were always held at 1:00 p.m. the next day. I go home and tell my wife the whole story. I'm sure I'll be fired.

"I never bothered to check on this guy at all; I've really messed things up."

After a sleepless night, I call Rikki Barr the next morning.

"Rikki, what happened?"

"What do you mean, what happened?"

"With Anatol Winagrodoff."

"What about him, isn't he a fine actor?"

"You didn't tell me that he couldn't speak English."

"You didn't ask."

"What about *Winterset*?"

"He learned the part phonetically."

"Thanks, Rikki!"

The dreaded one o'clock comes. Don Fedderson can't believe what he's hearing. "What is this? Who cast this guy?"

I sink down deeper and deeper into my seat. The dailies end. Fred Henry gets up. "Okay, what should we do? Go up to the top of the building and jump off?"

Don gives me a look. I'm thinking that he wants me to do the jumping. Fred saves the day. "Don, all we have to do is bring in someone to loop the guy's lines. No one will ever know."

Don is mollified. "Kid, you made a little mistake there, didn't you?"

Boy, did I.

LAS VEGAS WITH BOB ALTMAN

*T*here is nothing worse than doing a show with two costars who can't stand each other. When Ruta Lee and Rick Jason starred in an episode of *Millionaire*, it was hate at first sight. I have no idea what their problem with each other was. Sometimes when there is friction between actors, it will bring out energy between them. For example, William Frawley and Vivian Vance in *I Love Lucy*, or Tom Tully and Warner Anderson in *The Lineup*. This was not the case with Ruta Lee and Rick Jason. Especially during love scenes.

We'd shoot a master shot. This usually went fine. Then came the dreaded close-ups. Rick would be seated in a car, and Ruta would be outside the car in a very romantic scene. As we'd be shooting Ruta's close-up, Rick would speak his lines off-camera. Instead of looking at

Ruta or at least at the script, Rick would be pointedly reading the *Los Angeles Times*'s sports page. The situation was reversed when we were doing Rick's close-ups. Ruta would turn her back while she did her offstage lines and munch on a sandwich. They both came out of the show alive.

Another episode of *The Millionaire* was one we were to film in Las Vegas. DANGER! My great weakness was gambling. We made a deal with the Sands Hotel. Jack Entratter ran the Sands at that time. We were going to film in Vegas for two days and come back to the studio for one day. The Sands chartered an airplane, put us up in the hotel, fed us three meals a day, and paid all of the company's expenses. They couldn't have been nicer. In return for this, Jack Entratter asked for three things: the sign of the Sands to be displayed in the show, a credit after the show, and nothing in the script involving gangsters or the mob. We wholeheartedly agreed to the whole package.

Bob Altman (*the* Robert Altman), Sid Sidman, the assistant director, and I went to Las Vegas to scout locations. Mistake Number One: we went to Vegas three days ahead of time to get everything set up. Mistake Number Two: we got everything set up in three hours. Mistake Number Three: I was given $10,000 in cash for expense money to cover expenses for the cast and crew in Vegas. I didn't realize that Bob Altman *and* Sid Sidman also had gambling problems. Imagine three gamblers in Vegas with nothing to do for two-and-a-half days!

The first evening we split up, agreeing to meet for breakfast the next morning. Right away, I do what any good husband would do. I go to the hotel gift shop and, with my own money, buy my wife a gift. I take it up to my room. Then I immediately go down to where the action is. At about 2:30 a.m. I'm standing over the roulette table. I'm exhausted. I can't say that I'm broke, but I can say that the company's $10,000 is with the Sands Hotel and not with me.

Bob and Sid find me. They plead with me to loan them money. They've already gone through their per diem. I tell them about the $10,000.

"I have exactly two dollars of my own money left."

What am I to do? I do what any good gambler would do. I start calling my friends. First I call home. This is the first time my wife is exposed to this problem of mine (the first of many times). She tells me that all we have in our savings account is $2,000. Begrudgingly, she says she'll wire it up to me. I have to wait till morning to call some true friends. The first person I phone is Bernadette at the Desilu Credit Union. She's used to my calls. Then I make some other calls. By the time the crew shows up, I have the entire $10,000.

The story has spread rapidly. Fred Henry arrives. Here comes trouble. "Well, I've heard what you've done, what are you going to do about it?"

"Here, Fred, here's the whole $10,000. No problem."

It took me five years to pay everyone back.

Bob Altman was one of my many bad judgment calls. If you asked me about Bob Altman when I first started working with him on *The Millionaire*, I would have told you, "He'll never amount to anything."

Bob never changed. He would direct great scenes. He could improvise better then anyone. He was the best director for shooting *The Millionaire* openings. You could put him out in the freeway and tell him it was a desert.

"Okay, I'll make something out of it." He always did.

The least important thing to Bob was the script. In television it is vital to have a beginning, middle, and end. In features, the first huge hit Bob had was *M*A*S*H*. In movies, his way of making the scenes interesting scene by scene went over big. In TV, a scene has to follow the preceding scene to make sense. Bob's TV shows often strayed off course.

For example, in Las Vegas we're going out for the first shot of the show. Bob spots two young girls dressed in bikinis, sitting out on their porch sipping martinis. It's eight o'clock in the morning.

"John, this is great. Get the camera crew here quick, I want to shoot this."

"Bob, it's not in the script."

"John, it'll be fine." We get the camera crew and film the girls.

We shoot 25,000 feet in Las Vegas alone. Normal filming on a thirty-minute TV show was 10,000 feet. When we get back to L.A. there are maybe 500 feet of usable film. It's all on Andy Clyde walking his mule down a street in Las Vegas. We had been in Vegas mainly for that scene.

The Vegas episode airs. A major news event occurs in the United States. Not only are the end credits of *The Millionaire* deleted, to make matters worse, the final scene of Andy Clyde leaving the Sands Hotel, with its sign prominently displayed, is also deleted. There go two of the promises to the Sands. Jack Entratter is on the phone to me the next day. "What the hell happened?"

"I'm going to do something I don't have the power to do, but I promise you, it will be done."

"And just what is that?"

"I'll put the show on the rerun schedule and it will be run in its entirety, with nothing deleted. It's not my job, but I'll tell everyone what happened. I know they'll honor this. I'll call you back to confirm this."

Don Fedderson agrees to put the show on the summer rerun schedule. I call Jack Entratter back and tell him the summer rerun has been confirmed.

"It better be!"

Up comes the day the show is to be rerun. The entire show is pre-empted! I didn't take any phone calls that week.

One day while working on *The Millionaire*, I was sitting in the commissary at Desilu Cahuenga. Seated across from me was an elderly man I had seen for years playing character parts in movies. At this time he was playing Fred Mertz in *I Love Lucy*. William Frawley. He was dressed in a suit and tie, having soup. Actually his suit and tie were getting more of the soup then he was. I remember thinking, wow—he's still acting. I wonder how he ever gets through his lines. Never in a million years did I dream that I would soon be working with him.

Bill Frawley was the first person cast in *My Three Sons*.

HOW WE FILMED *MY THREE SONS*

*O*f all the shows I worked on at Don Fedderson, *My Three Sons* was my favorite. It was on the air from 1960 to 1972, and I was with the show for the whole run.

Bill Frawley had the same deal on *My Three Sons* that he had on *I Love Lucy*. His agent, Walter Meyers, insisted on this. He was paid residuals into perpetuity, which was very unusual. In those days, residuals ended after six shows. Bill would get residuals for all reruns of *I Love Lucy* and *My Three Sons*. They still go to his estate to this day.

After Bill was cast, we went for Fred MacMurray. First he said yes. Then he said no. He told Don Fedderson that he had spoken to Robert Young. Young told him that television was great, but the hours were absolutely murder. On the set at eight o'clock in the morning, home at ten o'clock at night. The money was great, but who wanted to go through that grind? Strangely, while Young was telling Fred this he was doing a television series, and he wound up doing two more.

Then we got lucky. I remembered Sid Sidman and Carl Nugent, who had been at MGM, telling me that Clark Gable's deal with the studio after he came back from the service was 8:30 a.m. to 5:00 p.m. Out at five o'clock, no matter what. Everybody at MGM knew this. If they were lining up a big shot at three-thirty, Clark Gable would ask the cameraman, "Think you'll roll on this by five?" If the cameraman said "no," that was the end of the day for Gable.

I discussed the idea with Don, who explained that eight-thirty to five o'clock wouldn't be practical for a television show. We compromised: 8:30 a.m. to 6:30 p.m. Sixty-five days to complete thirty-nine episodes. Anything over sixty-five days, Fred would be paid $5,000 per day. Fred agreed to this.

Since we had thirty-nine shows to do, before the start of filming, we needed twenty-six completed "ready to shoot" scripts. Later, when we were reduced to twenty-six shows, we had to have sixteen completed scripts. In today's world of studios and networks getting involved in everything, TV shows are lucky if they have two shooting scripts in the bank at any time.

Each script began with a time and day of the week. Many Broadway plays did this. For instance, a script might start "Tuesday at 7:00 a.m." and the fourth scene might read "the following Friday at 8:00 p.m." This would keep wardrobe straight, along with props and dialogue. All of the actors had to know their character and always play that character. We couldn't use any Actors Studio types. Sometimes we'd shoot the master shot, three weeks later do three shots, and two weeks after that do close-ups.

Fred MacMurray's deal changed in the second season of *My Three Sons*. In season one it was 8:30 a.m. to 6:30 p.m. and sixty-five days. In season two it was 8:30 a.m. to 5:00 p.m., forty-five days and no Fridays. Fred did his own makeup, and 8:30 a.m. meant he was ready to start filming at 8:30 a.m.

We had only one director, one assistant director, one director of photography, and one prop master. There was no doubling up on any crew positions. This was essential. We had one script supervisor and a dialogue coach. The dialogue coach would do all the offstage lines for the minors and usually for Fred. We had a still photographer on the set at all times. He took Polaroids to match wardrobe, set dressing, etc. It was vital that we started to film in March for a September airdate.

If Fred was working on a feature, we'd start shooting without him. We'd do all the scenes that he wasn't in until he became available. Just before his arrival, we'd do two "swing shows." We'd finish these two shows without Fred and then when Fred came in, we'd finish Fred's part of the shows. If it worked the other way around, we'd shoot all of Fred's parts and then do two swing shows finishing without Fred. We made a deal with the Screen Actors Guild so we didn't have to pay for the guest actors' intervening times. However, their return date had to be at their convenience. Before airdates, we'd usually have sixteen shows in the can.

During Fred's days we would concentrate on Fred. After Fred left for the day, we would go to close-ups of the guest stars without Fred there, or we'd film the kids. The guest stars would often do their close-ups with the dialogue coach doing Fred's dialogue and anyone else's in the scene. If necessary, members of the crew would hold up mops and brooms to give the guest star spots to look at to match the master. Occasionally, this would become difficult for the actor, but Fred, bless him, if he had been working that day, would often stay around (up to a point) and do his own offstage dialogue.

We always shot with two cameras: one camera on the master shot including Fred and one on Fred's close-up. If the script called for Fred to be on location, we'd finish that location and not return to it. However, to add to production values, we'd try to make these shows our swing shows.

Often, returning actors would have a mismatch problem with hair or makeup. Vera Miles had completed her part with Fred and was due to return to us for one day. She was doing a Disney film and had a day off. She called me the night before coming back to us.

"John, my hair is red, not brown, and it's very short. I know you have to shoot my over-the-shoulders over Fred's double on to me and then my close-ups. It won't match any of the two-shots that I've already done with Fred in the same scene."

"Vera, don't worry, nobody will notice it."
They never did.

We only had one stage on which to film. Since we had numerous sets we would often have to shoot all the parts of episodes we had scripts for in one set to make room for other sets. The house bathroom was always the first to go. There were never any outside actors working in our bathroom. Once we filmed parts of thirteen episodes in our bathroom in one day. Fred wasn't too happy about this. If an outside actor was in the bathroom, we would rewrite the scene. Fedderson's rules were simple. You could change sets as long as it didn't affect the story.

We had a Moviola on the set at all times to match intricate crosses and left-to-right entrances and exits. Actually, with the exception of shooting around the star, the whole concept of how we shot *My Three Sons* was based on the way they used to film serials. In most respects this way of filming, believe it or not, was easier than the conventional way. We weren't under the gun regarding airdates, and if we didn't complete a scene on Monday, we could get it three weeks from next Tuesday.

There were certain strict rules: no hairstyle changes within the day; no more than one wardrobe change per day; no changing of dialogue once the master shot was completed. All twenty-six (or sixteen) shows were on a production board in a production office. This way we had the luxury of changing schedules if necessary. Absolutely no one could question the schedule. Of course, this was my rule. If somebody died before their return, we'd ignore it. If we had already shot the master scene with that actor, there would be no coverage of them. This actually happened to us once.

If somebody broke an arm or leg, this was serious. Since we filmed *Family Affair* in much the same way, we encountered the broken leg problem on that show with Anissa Jones. During filming, Anissa broke her leg. We had a stunt double walk into each scene for her. Once set, we'd put Anissa into the scene, always having her cast blocked by a piece of set dressing—chair, table, whatever. Once her leg got better, we returned to our normal shooting style. Then, horror of horrors, she rebroke the leg. Since we'd never mentioned it in the show before, and to say we filmed out of continuity would be putting it mildly, we returned to the stunt double and the furniture. Also, Anissa did a lot of sitting.

There were no production meetings on *My Three Sons*. I would meet every Tuesday or Wednesday with the director and the first assistant director (AD) for an hour. We would go over the next week's schedule, and the first AD would pass on pertinent information to the crew. It was essential that the schedule for the next week's filming listed every detail needed for each and every scene.

I always wondered about *My Three Sons* being overlooked at Emmy time. Fred MacMurray never even received an Emmy nomination in our twelve years. Oh well, Tramp, the dog on *My Three Sons*, did win two Patsys [these are awards similar to an Oscar for animals who've done outstanding performances in TV and movies]. Hollywood figured there had to be something strange about the way our show was filmed. They just didn't understand. How could we ever be deserving of an Emmy? The public disagreed. We were seldom out of the top ten in the Nielsen ratings and never out of the top twenty, even though they kept moving our time slot. We prevailed until they moved us to eight-thirty Thursday night opposite the last half hour of *The Flip Wilson Show*.

CASTING *MY THREE SONS*

*O*nce we'd cast Bill Frawley as Uncle Bub and Fred as the father, Steve Douglas, we started in on the rest of the casting. This process was started with no director. I was in charge of the preliminary casting. Don Fedderson would okay all the people.

The very first person who came into my office was Stanley Livingston. His opening remark was, "My name is Stanley Livingston and no cracks!" That impressed me, as did his reading. I interviewed a few other actors, but only took Stanley to meet Don Fedderson. Once Don met Stanley, he didn't want to meet anyone else. Stanley became Chip.

Originally the part of the second son, Robbie, was to be played by Bobby Diamond. Bobby's deal wasn't finalized, and we ran into a number of problems with him on the first day of rehearsal.

We cast the role of Mike, the third son, with Ryan O'Neal, who impressed both Don Fedderson and myself. Ryan had just come back from doing a syndicated series with his father. He was good-looking and clean-cut. We felt that Stanley, Bobby, and Ryan would be perfect.

We then got the director, Peter Tewksbury. Peter had worked with Ryan on *Father Knows Best*. He hadn't been pleased with Ryan. After the first day's rehearsal, Peter announced that he wanted a meeting with Fred, Don, and me.

"I've just fired Ryan O'Neal. He's a terrible actor. You guys make it official. Pay him whatever you have to, but fire him."

This was Peter showing his authority. I only worked with him for one year. It seemed like five. However, I have to say he was the person most responsible for setting the tone of *My Three Sons*.

Bobby Diamond and his agent were waiting to see us after the meeting. Bobby's agent told us that Bobby was happy with the show, but he insisted on two-and-a-half percent of the profits. Don Fedderson bid Bobby and his agent good-bye. Here we were, going into the second day of rehearsal looking for two of the three sons.

We brought in a number of people during the lunch hour to read for the role of Robbie, and we decided to bring in actors to read for the role of Mike when we finished rehearsal that night. One of the four boys we brought in to read for Robbie was Don Grady. He came in with his mother, Mary Grady, who was also his agent. She reminded me that during my preliminary interviews, I wouldn't even see Don.

"Mary, he was a Mouseketeer. We want actors."

Don gave a sensational reading. Peter Tewksbury hired him on the spot.

In the evening four actors came in to read for the role of Mike. Tim Considine got the part. We had our cast: Fred MacMurray, William Frawley, Tim Considine, Don Grady, and Stanley Livingston.

We started filming the pilot in June. It was called *Chip Off the Old Block*. The show was a "family-com." A lot of humor. No one-line jokes. Peter Tewksbury was in charge of everything. He was in fact the producer, director, story editor, writer, casting director, music editor, and sound editor. Peter's day would start at five o'clock in the morning and would end around three o'clock the next morning. He was an absolutely tireless worker. We had very long shooting hours. We only had three adults on the show: Fred MacMurray, Bill Frawley, and Tim Considine. Fred would only work until 6:30 p.m. Bill would collapse around three o'clock in the afternoon. We would shoot all of Tim's close-ups and the adult guest cast well into the night.

Peter was an absolute perfectionist to the point that he would drive the rest of us crazy. He wanted the house to look like five males lived in it. There was always clutter around, and nothing was neat; exactly the way five men would live. One of the things that drove Peter nuts was that Bill Frawley had to be the cook and housekeeper. I doubt if Bill had ever boiled water in his life.

Bill would always be making a salad. Instead of chopping the lettuce with a knife, he'd grab the lettuce with his hands and throw it around. We'd have to keep cutting away from this. Then he'd be making a stew. Instead of slicing the carrots, he'd attack them as if he were sawing wood. Strangely, no one in our audience ever noticed.

We did have something very interesting in the kitchen where the family ate their meals. It was Peter's idea to have a "lazy Susan" built and put in the middle of the kitchen table. All the food went around so the family didn't have to say "Can I have this or that." It saved us a lot of time when they would spin it around to get their eggs or whatever Bill Frawley had supposedly cooked. We got a lot of mail from people asking where they could buy a lazy Susan like the one in our kitchen.

We worked long days and nights. The crew became exhausted. We probably had, age-wise, the oldest crew in Hollywood. Our crew averaged about seventy-five years of age. I realized early on that I knew absolutely nothing about production. I hired the best people I could find and learned from them. There was nothing that ever came up that they hadn't been through, and there were so many things in production that I had never been through. We balanced things out by having the older people train younger people. For example, Sid Sidman, the first assistant director, had as the second assistant a young fellow, Sheldon Schrager. Schrager went on to become the head of a studio and a well-known producer. Also, our assistant prop master, assistant camera people, etc., were all young.

We got lucky because at that time movies were in a little bit of a slump, and television was starting to make big inroads. A lot of people from the old MGM days were available. I was told by many people that our older crew wouldn't be able to work fast. That just wasn't true. They were just as fast as they had to be. They had done a lot of features at MGM in seventeen and eighteen days. We had people who had won Academy Awards: Paul Vogel for *Battleground*, Bob Planck who was nominated a number of times, and, as I mentioned earlier, Sid Sidman, and Carl Nugent. What seems to be the case today is that young fellows get their chance and bring in a bunch of their friends. They bumble and stumble along, learning as they go. When we hired young people, they were young people who had been trained under older, experienced people.

The crew was really funny. They would complain bitterly about the late hours. They would grumble and mumble and they'd smoke and they'd cough. They'd smoke and they'd cough.

The next morning their call would be seven-thirty for an eight o'-clock shooting. I'd get into the office at 5:30 a.m. and around six or so, I would go to the commissary for coffee. I'd find the coughers there, eating breakfast and coughing and smoking and smoking and coughing. Probably *My Three Sons* could have been done even faster if we hadn't had so many takes interrupted by coughs. We probably set the record for cough-interrupted takes!

I would make certain suggestions to Peter, and he would tell me they were great. I'd go back to my office proud that I'd finally made some points with him. Twenty-five minutes later there would be a memo from Peter saying that everything I'd said was stupid, idiotic, and wrong. When I'd follow his orders, like setting up at a certain house he had suggested, he'd walk over and say, "No, no that's the wrong house. I want the one across the street."

Two things about Peter. He was always at the location before any of us, and his choice of locations was usually right.

The first season of *My Three Sons* went way over schedule and way over budget. Fred MacMurray worked twenty-five extra days at $5,000 a day, which in those days was a goodly amount of money. One of the reasons for this was that Peter insisted on total reality.

We were going to do a scene where Bill Frawley walks into a shoe store to buy a pair of shoes and comes out with the shoe box under his arm. We have a shoe store set on the stage. They rehearse the scene. Bill walks into the store, picks out a pair of shoes, and leaves with the shoe box under his arm. A simple scene. Peter asks if the shoes in the box are actually Mr. Frawley's? No, they aren't. He says the scene won't work then, because an actor can only relate to the scene if he knows he's carrying shoes in his size in the shoe box. It's ten o'clock at night. Peter tells me to send a driver to Bill Frawley's house to get a pair of his shoes, bring them back, and place them inside the box he's carrying out. This way he can relate to the shoes. That's what we did. Bear in mind that

Bill Frawley was hardly a "method" actor and couldn't have cared less whose shoes were in the box, or indeed if *anything* was in the box.

We would shoot all scenes with Fred MacMurray three ways. We'd shoot the scene the way the script was written, then we'd shoot it Peter's way, and then we'd shoot it Fred's way. What Fred didn't realize was that Peter edited the shows, so the final version of the show was always Peter's way.

Don Fedderson was not used to doing shows that lost any money. Although *My Three Sons* was often number one, and always in the top ten in the ratings, the costs of doing the episodes kept skyrocketing. Don, Fred Henry, and I had a number of meetings to discuss what could be done to bring the costs under control. In these meetings, I explained all of the things that Peter Tewksbury had been doing which I felt were the biggest contributors to the problem.

One Friday night at eleven o'clock Don calls a meeting that turns out to be the last straw between Peter and me. Peter, Fred Henry, and I join Don in his office. Don starts the meeting by saying, "Peter, we're over schedule, we're over budget, we can't afford this, and John Stephens says every bit of it is your fault."

I'm shrinking into my seat thinking about having to work with this guy for another twenty shows. Peter looks at me. "Don, let me think about that."

On Monday, Peter sends a ten-page memo to Don, addressed "To Don Fedderson Only," in which he blames everything on me, claiming I'm going to low-budget us out of the top ten. Don sends copies to Fred Henry and me.

We have a meeting at the end of the season. Don gives us the good news. "Peter Tewksbury is not coming back next season. Fred MacMurray is delighted with the success of the show and is definitely coming back."

Fred MacMurray was the best actor and star I ever had the pleasure of working with.

FRED'S FRUGALITY

*L*et's get all of the stories you've heard about Fred MacMurray out of the way. First, his frugality. I'm going to a prizefight one time with Fred,

Bill Frawley and his driver Phil Tanner, Gene Reynolds the director, Sid Sidman, and Carl Nugent. The fight is going to be shown live on a big screen at the Pantages Theater. First we go to Nickodell's, a well-known restaurant at the time, for dinner. At Nickodell's we meet Cissy Wellman, daughter of the famous Hollywood director, William Wellman. She's a fun gal, an actress, who would hang around the set and had worked on a few *My Three Sons*. We finish dinner, and the waitress presents the check to Fred, who proceeds to go down each item and tell us what we owe.

"John, you owe $3.75 and thirty-five cents for the tip."

And so on. We aren't surprised and give him the money. I get a little gutsy and say, "Fred, don't you think you could at least pay for Cissy Wellman?"

"Absolutely not, her father has plenty of money; she can pay her own way like everyone else!"

We get to the Pantages Theater parking lot. The parking fee is two dollars. As we pull in, Fred looks at us—there are eight of us—and says, "That'll be twenty-five cents apiece."

On the way in to the theater, Fred gives Carl Nugent a quarter and tells him to buy a fifty-cent candy bar. "We'll split it."

We get to our seats and the fight starts. Wham. Bam. Fight's over, knockout in the first round! Fred has a fit.

"John, you never told me this would happen. I paid good money for my ticket!"

"How could I know this would happen? It's a one-round knockout. That happens at prizefights."

Fred mutters all the way home about wasting his money.

Fred and I bet on a football game. I pick USC, and he picks Notre Dame. We bet a whole dollar. The game is on a Saturday and at the end of the first half, USC is ahead twenty-eight to zero. Fred calls me at home.

"John, the score is twenty-eight to nothing."

"I know, boy, I can really use that dollar."

"Well, that's why I'm calling. I'd like to settle for fifty cents right now."

"No way, Fred, I want the whole dollar."

Now this is not the end of this story, and here's where I learned a valuable lesson. I wait for Fred to come in on Monday, and I go to the set where they're in rehearsal. When they break, I say, "Fred you owe me a dollar, and don't call me anymore and try to settle for fifty cents at halftime when you're twenty-eight points behind."

Fred didn't laugh.

He was right, and I was wrong. Never embarrass anyone in front of others. It's a lesson I've never forgotten.

Fred De Cordova, a later *My Three Sons* director, was a very generous man. He was probably the most generous man in show business. Fred De Cordova always asked what you would like for Christmas. He knew that Joan and I liked nice restaurants, so he gave us gift certificates to the Bistro Gardens and to *the* restaurant of those days, Chasen's.

For our anniversary, I said to Joan that maybe we should use the gift certificate De Cordova had given us and go to Chasen's for dinner. Joan agreed and called for reservations. The night of our anniversary, we're looking forward to this wonderful dinner we'll have at Chasen's. When we arrive, the maître d takes us on a trek through the place to a table at the far side of the restaurant, almost out the back door. Of course we're both upset. We didn't expect the best table, but we thought we'd at least be seated at a decent table. I go to the phone and call De Cordova but he isn't home. Then I remember that Fred MacMurray has told me on many occasions about being close personal friends with Dave and Maude Chasen, the owners. I call Fred and tell him what's happened.

"John, don't leave the table."

I go back to Joan and tell her what Fred has said. About five minutes later, Maude Chasen comes to our table.

"Ahhh, Mr. and Mrs. Stephens, there has been a terrible mistake, please follow me."

She proceeds to usher us not just to the front of the restaurant, but to the best table in the restaurant, as another couple is being unceremoniously moved to a different table. All of a sudden a waiter appears with a bottle of champagne, compliments of Fred and June MacMurray. We're enjoying the champagne and waiting for our meal when Maude comes up to our table.

"Excuse me, but who exactly are you and what do you do?"

"I'm John Stephens, the production manager on *My Three Sons*."

"Well, Dave and I have known Fred MacMurray for years, and he's never bought anyone anything, let alone a bottle of champagne. We figured you had to be very important people. A production manager?"

Fred MacMurray was a talented actor and appeared in many great films. He worked on the motion picture *The Apartment* during a *My Three Sons* hiatus. After the movie was released, he was at Disneyland when two old ladies came up to him and started swatting him with their purses saying, "Shame on you! How could Steve Douglas [Fred's character name in *My Three Sons*] ever play a person as mean as the one in *The Apartment*? Don't you ever make a movie like that again."

He never did!

Fred had a habit of changing every word in every script. Everything had to be completely accurate, or he didn't want to do it. In one episode, the eldest son in the show, Mike, has a girlfriend. The girlfriend has a crush on Mike's father. Mike and the girl are driving to some lover's lane type of place for youngsters, and the girl is asking all these questions about Mr. Douglas.

The next day, Mr. Douglas is in his office and gets a phone call from the girl. Immediately Fred MacMurray shouts, "Stop, get John Stephens down here!" (I don't know why he didn't ask for the writer or producer.)

I rush down to the set.

"John, this scene here—how did this girl get my phone number? How can there be a scene where she calls me up? Don't tell me she got my number out of the phone book because she doesn't know where I work."

"Fred, you aren't here for every scene. If you look through the whole script, you'll see where Mike was with the girl right after she met you. Can't we assume she asked Mike where you worked and that's how she got the number?"

With everything Fred would do, he would insist on putting a handle on it. If someone were throwing pebbles at Robbie's window, Fred would come to the window.

"Hi, you want Robbie? Well, he's not here. Now you're probably wondering why I'm here. It's because knowing Robbie wasn't here, I wanted to make sure his bed was made."

Things like that. What Fred didn't realize was what happened in the editing room . . . snip, snip, snip.

This happened during season one on *My Three Sons*. The company at that time was doing a show in New York called *Who Do You Trust?* starring Johnny Carson. And out here in California, we were doing *The Lawrence Welk Show*, *The Liberace Show*, and *My Three Sons*. Someone in the company had an idea to make one master Christmas list instead of breaking it down into individual shows. This list included every single person who worked on every single show. All in all, the list was between fifteen and seventeen pages long. Someone gave that list to Fred Mac-Murray. I must say that Fred really went overboard for the *My Three Sons* show. He gave each of us beautiful gold cuff links with the *My Three Sons* logo (the three pairs of feet) on them and a beautiful tie clasp to match.

About a month later, I was on the set and Fred said, "John, about that Christmas list . . . "

"What? I thanked you already."

"Yes, you thanked me. Also about 300 other people I've never heard of thanked me! Who are these people from New York and these people from *Liberace*? I got the Christmas list and assumed you had made it. I sent gifts to all these people. John, in the future, you make out the list and do one only for *My Three Sons*. Do you understand?"

FROM BILL FRAWLEY TO BILL DEMAREST

*B*ill Frawley was a great guy. They don't make people like him anymore. When Bill took a liking to you, you couldn't shake him. We'd go to the local restaurant, Nickodell's, every day for lunch with a whole group. Bill wanted me there for one reason. He wanted to talk about the old sports figures, and he knew I was up on that. That's why he'd drag me along, to answer sports questions.

"Johnny, who was it that played shortstop for the Hollywood Stars again?"

"Joe Hoover."

"That's right."

I remember the last time Bill ever went to Nickodell's. We finish lunch and he takes the check. He looks at the bill and says, angrily and loudly, "What? Old Fashioneds have gone from eighty-five cents to ninety-five cents? Why?! I'll never come in here again!"

He paid the check and never went into Nickodell's again.

I get a call from Don Fedderson one afternoon to tell me that Ralph Edwards of *This Is Your Life* wants to do Bill's story. I have to go to the Vine Street Brown Derby to be with Bill until Edwards comes to get him. Bill knows nothing about it. We're at the Derby, having a few drinks of course, when Ralph Edwards shows up with his camera crew. Bill, after a few drinks, was not the most gracious man. As a matter of fact, *without* a few drinks he wasn't the most gracious man. When Edwards walks over, cameras rolling, and introduces himself, Bill says, "What the hell is this?"

Ralph Edwards explains everything, and we get Bill out of there.

I guarantee you that had to have been the funniest *This Is Your Life* ever. With every person who comes on, Bill says, "No, I don't remember you. No, I don't remember that." They bring out high school teachers, people he had worked with, and people he hated. The worst thing they do is bring on Bill's ex-wife. He'd only been married once in his life, and he couldn't stand the lady. You could see the look on Bill's face as he nearly passed out. I'm sure there was a lot of editing of the words that came out of Bill's mouth on that show. It was a total disaster.

My wife was doing an episode of *My Three Sons*. Bill knew her very well. He would always say, "John, if it wasn't for Joan, you'd be in the gutter." Words that were brought up to me many times by Joan during our forty-two years of marriage! He was probably right.

The day Joan's episode is filming, she phones me in my office and suggests I come down to the set because she feels that Bill is having some kind of a problem. When I get to the set, Joan tells me to go into Bill's dressing room and talk to him. I find Bill and ask him how things are going.

"Hey John, have you seen that redhead on the set? Boy, would I like to fuck her."

"Bill! Do you know who that is, Bill?"

"Oh no, is that Joan?"

"Yes, it is, Bill."

"Forget that I said that."

Bill had a driver, Phil Tanner, whom he browbeat constantly. Phil was almost like Bill's stooge. Bill gave him $250 a week to drive him everywhere. I get a call from Bill one night. "John, ya know what that damn Tanner did to me?"

"No, what?"

"He died!"

I was the only one allowed to take Bill for his yearly physical. The actors had to have insurance and could only get insured if they passed their physicals. Every year we would go see Dr. Gerson who would pass anybody. If you were breathing, he'd pass you. This year, Dr. Gerson asked to speak to me after Bill's physical.

"John, I've always done whatever I could for you, but I can't pass Bill. He should have been dead two years ago. There isn't anything a human being can have that Bill doesn't have, and he has them in spades."

I didn't tell Bill what Dr. Gerson had told me. When I got back to the office, I immediately went to tell Don Fedderson what the doctor had said. We tried everywhere to get Bill insured because we shot the shows out of order and to have the costar die would be a disaster. It was decided to gamble that Bill would be okay to finish the season. I had to tell Bill about not being able to get him insured and that we would have to let him go after completing his thirteen episodes of season four. It was a tough thing to do. He didn't take it well.

William Demarest followed Bill Frawley on *My Three Sons*. We attempted to make the transition without the two of them ever encountering each other. Unfortunately, Bill Demarest showed up a day earlier than he was supposed to. It was a rather ugly scene on the set. Probably the only one we ever had on the set of *My Three Sons*. Frawley complained bitterly about leaving the show. He wanted to stay, and Demarest didn't know what to make of it. It seems that Frawley and Demarest had been up for a number of the same parts throughout their careers. Finally Frawley was finished for the day. Demarest went to wardrobe for a fitting and reported the next day.

Bill Demarest was in his seventies also, but was a little more agile in the kitchen than was Bill Frawley. He could stay awake and remember his lines. He was in extremely good condition for a man of his age.

He lived well into his nineties. Bill Demarest had done a number of large roles in a lot of big features at MGM and Paramount. He could do everything—he could dance, he could sing, and he was a real trooper. He wasn't Bill Frawley, though; no one will ever be.

I would recommend that anyone interested in *My Three Sons* try and get a copy of the issue of *Spy Magazine* where they did the great piece on the show. How people came in and out and disappeared. How Bill Frawley, a man in his eighties, was supposedly going to visit his mother in Ireland, who would have had to be in her hundreds. How Bill Demarest just happened to show up all of a sudden. He had never been mentioned before. How Bryant Park, the fictional town where our show took place, was a small Midwestern town with a large Chinatown, an ocean, an international airport, and a big football stadium. Whatever we wanted was in Bryant Park.

Bill Demarest caught on to a little trick I used to pull, and he called me on it. "John, this dance number we're doing? How come all of the tough stuff I have to do physically is always the last day of every season? Are you trying to tell me that if I die, you want me to die on the last day so you can put whatever I did together? Is that what you're trying to do?"

We didn't want him to die, of course, but yes, it was definitely true. That was wrong, that was mean, but that was life, and that's what we did.

Bill Demarest did not get along with the kids on the show as well as Bill Frawley did. Frawley may have been a cantankerous old guy, but he loved kids and got along great with them. Bill Demarest was much more of a professional, and he was a lot tougher on kids. They really didn't take to him the way they did to Bill Frawley. I have fond memories of both of them.

THREE SONS DIRECTORS

The second season we hired Dick Whorf to direct. He was a well-known actor and director from Warner Bros. and MGM. Dick, unfortunately, was not a well man and was not aware of how *My Three Sons* was filmed. He just couldn't catch on to all of the out-of-sequence filming. He also agreed with MacMurray on everything. While Fred was right about things a lot of times, a lot of times he wasn't. If a scene was set up in front of the house, Fred would say, "Shouldn't this be shot in the driveway?"

Dick would say, "Absolutely, in the driveway, get the cameras in the driveway."

Then Fred would say, "No, let's forget the drive up and have me just enter the house."

"Absolutely, enter the house." It became almost impossible to get scenes shot in the allotted time.

I'll never forget an episode where the script called for us to go on location. We had picked out Franklin Canyon. It was Saturday. We were going to have a boat on the lake and have Fred MacMurray leading a Boy Scout troop to the lake. We wanted Dick to see the locations. We bring him to Franklin Canyon, and he looks around.

"I don't understand, where do you see the putting green?"

"The putting green?"

Well, of course, Dick had brought the wrong script.

There were a number of times when Dick was ill and had to leave the set during filming. One of these times brought about my one and only experience of directing the first unit, so to speak. I tell Fred, "Dick is sick. It's Wednesday, so I can finish out the week directing."

Fred replies, "Fine, I'll be helping you."

"Please don't help me too much. Joan Blondell is our guest star this week. She'll be here tomorrow for two days. Please, Fred, don't be rewriting the script as we go along. If you have any changes, give them to me tonight, and I'll sit in your trailer and go over them with you."

"Oh no, John, everything is fine, no problems at all."

The next morning we're in rehearsal and right away, Fred starts changing the dialogue. I remind him of our conversation. Fine. We get a good rehearsal. The scene takes place in a grocery store. Fred and Joan meet in the store. We start.

"Just a minute, that's not the way June would do that [June Haver, a former actress and Fred's wife]. When she'd be looking in her purse, she wouldn't just look in her purse and pull out her list. She'd actually go through every compartment before finding it, or she might say, 'Oh, the list is in my hand.' Isn't that a good idea?"

"Not really, we don't have the time to have her looking through every compartment in her purse. That would be like a two-minute stage wait."

"We should do it anyway."

"Fred, June is not the guest star in the show, Joan Blondell is."

"Let's do it my way."

The whole day goes like this, and I drive home shaking my head. The next day, more of the same. Who directed the show? I guess we both did. That night Fred calls me. "John, did I give you any trouble?"

"Fred, absolutely not, I could never have gotten through it without you."

Following season two, we brought in Gene Reynolds as director for season three. The kids just adored him. He had been a child actor under contract to MGM, and was in *Boys Town* and a number of other big films. He really understood acting and understood the kids. He was with us for three seasons. The shows ran very smoothly with him.

After Gene Reynolds came probably my favorite director, Jimmy Kern (remember *Date with the Angels?*). One day I show him a set that is supposedly New York, walking down Fifth Avenue. It's on Stage Nine at Desilu Gower. Otto Preminger had built the whole street for *The Man with the Golden Arm.*

"Jimmy, this is Fifth Avenue."

Jimmy, who had been all over the world, says, "This is Fifth Avenue? John, do you want it good, or do you want it Wednesday?"

Jim, as Don Fedderson would say, "Get it as good as you can get it, but make sure you get it on Wednesday."

The only problem I ever had with Jimmy Kern was when we were on location during lunch. His wife, Ethel, would make him a pitcher of Bloody Marys. They were really strong. I didn't drink much even in the evenings, and I never drank at work or at lunch. I would actually hide in a trailer somewhere at lunchtime. Our second assistant, Mort Singer, at Jimmy Kern's request, would track me down and take me to where Jimmy was to join him for Bloody Marys. I would have one and if he poured me a second, I would find some way to get rid of it without his knowledge. Jimmy was a great guy and a lot of fun to be around.

The next director to come on the scene was Fred De Cordova. He put a lot of vigor back into the show. De Cordova was a unique man. He not only energized me, but the entire cast and crew as well. Fred came to Hollywood in the 1930s and should be in the *Guinness Book of World Records* for drawing continuous weekly salary checks from the East Coast to Hollywood, receiving them until his death in 2001. Fred had a sharp wit and was very clever. He was the only director we ever had who could talk so fast that after we did a shot with MacMurray, while Fred was wondering about it, De Cordova was already set up for the next shot. De Cordova was actually able to convince MacMurray that the shot was absolutely perfect and to go on to the next one.

The only thing pertaining to Fred De Cordova that we dreaded was on Monday morning reading about any social affairs in the *Hollywood Reporter* or *Daily Variety*. The problem was this: if Fred and his wife, Janet, had attended some big party over the weekend, and it was mentioned in the trades, the worst thing that could happen was if all the celebrities were listed in the story, and at the end of the list it said "*and* Fred and Janet De Cordova." Then all hell would break loose.

Another uniqueness about Fred De Cordova was that he could eat lunch one day at the Bistro, a very posh, "in" restaurant in Beverly Hills, and the next day have lunch at the counter of a Thrifty Drug Store in the Valley.

I went to the racetrack with him once. He took me to the paddock and introduced me to Bill Shoemaker, the famous jockey. While we were talking to "the Shoe" he gave us tips on three horses, and I remember thinking, "Bill Shoemaker giving us tips on horses. They'll never lose." As far as I know, they're still running.

De Cordova and I were always teasing each other and playing jokes on one another. One year, I add a note to the schedule saying that at the end of filming, there would be a cast and crew party at Fred and Janet's. R.S.V.P. Fred goes bananas.

"Everybody at CBS knows me, and everybody is calling Janet saying they'll be there. She didn't know what was going on and called me, but I didn't know either. Then I saw the schedule that had been sent around. Who could have done this thing?"

Well, he finds out it was me, and a couple of days later while I'm off the lot at a meeting, he has signs posted around the lot. Fred has signs put up in the commissary, in restrooms, anywhere they can't be missed, saying that the address for the Friday night party has been changed to accommodate the large turnout expected, and he's put my address on the signs. We really had some great laughs.

Fred and I also did a pilot at Fedderson, *To Rome with Love*. We filmed a large portion of it in Rome. Mike Joyce, the cameraman, and I got to Italy a little early. We were scouting locations to show to Fred. We were supposed to pick Fred up at the airport. I call the airport to say we're on our way but traffic is heavy so we're running late.

"Don't worry about that, but make sure you have a hospital I can go to. I'm very, very sick."

Well, we're always playing jokes on each other, so I kind of laugh about it. When we get to the airport, I take one look at Fred and see that he really is sick. We get him to a doctor who gives him a shot and says he should go to bed. We put him to bed, and he sleeps all afternoon and evening. He gets up the next morning feeling fine. Along with never missing a paycheck, I doubt if he missed one day of work, ever, from being sick. That's the kind of guy he was.

JIMMY STEWART AT SCALE

$\mathcal{O}$ne of the more amusing things that happened with celebrities on *My Three Sons* concerned Jimmy Stewart. An episode we did portrayed Robbie as an egghead, getting all A's in his classes and being teased by the other kids for being such a good student. What we needed on that episode was a celebrity, if we could get one, to come in and give a one-day, eight-minute speech, about nine pages of dialogue, explaining to the class how important it was to study. This was during the time the United States was putting our first men into space. It was very important to us. First we tried for John Glenn, who was unavailable. We tried for a number of the other astronauts who were also unavailable.

A gentleman whom I knew very well and had worked with a lot, Major Eugene Albert, was the head of the Hollywood film office for the Air Force. He's in my office one day, and I tell him about our situation to see if he knows anybody who might be available to us. "How would ya like Jimmy Stewart?"

"We'd like Jimmy Stewart, but we're not going to get Jimmy Stewart."

"Just a minute. Jimmy Stewart has to spend fifteen days assigned to the United States Air Force. During those fifteen days, he's our property, and we can assign him to anything we want. He has no say in the matter."

"Well, I . . . ah . . . we can't . . . I mean . . . Jimmy Stewart . . . also we can't pay him . . . "

"You can't pay him, that's right."

"I mean we can't pay him the money he'd want."

"No, you can't pay him, period! He's the property of the United States Air Force."

"But this is Jimmy Stewart . . . "

"He'll have no choice."

"We have to pay him scale, $70 a day, because of his union."

"That'll be fine."

Everyone is very excited that we're going to have Jimmy Stewart on our show. I tell Fred MacMurray, who's a little dubious because he and Jimmy Stewart are friends. I explain what Major Albert had told me. About a week later I get a phone call from Major Albert saying it's all set with Jimmy Stewart. He's assigned to the show and wants the script sent to him. I send him the script. I get a phone call from Mr. Stewart himself saying fine, he'd love to be there, and he'll definitely do it. He only asks for a couple of changes in the script, plugging the United States Air Force Academy, which is fine with us. He calls me a few days before he's scheduled to work and gives me the names of the people he wants on the set with him: his makeup man, his stand-in, and a couple of others. The day of the shoot, Mr. Stewart arrives, goes into makeup, reports to the set, and every single shot is one take. We finish the episode. It's unbelievable—Jimmy Stewart guest starring in *My Three Sons*! *And* for $70 a day.

The show airs. It's a big success. Two months later, I get a call from Jimmy Stewart's agent, who had been out of town at the time of filming. To say he's flipping out is putting it mildly.

"Who do you think you are? You should be running Hollywood! You got Jimmy Stewart for $70 a day?"

"Look, he was in the Air Force, they assigned him to our show, and we couldn't pay him more."

"That's not the point, you've got to do something about this. Jimmy seems to recall you mentioning something about a $20,000 donation to the Air Force Academy in his name. I want that done right away."

I tell him I never mentioned that. He says I did. We have a meeting with Jimmy Stewart, his agent, Don Fedderson, Fred Henry, and Major Albert. Jimmy Stewart and his agent present their case. Jimmy Stewart says that maybe I didn't actually say it, but that he just took it for granted that something would be done for the United States Air Force Academy. His agent pipes up, "Yes, like at least a $20,000 donation in Jimmy Stewart's name."

Major Albert says, "We love the Academy, naturally, but that was not any part of this deal at all. As far as I'm concerned, John is right, the deal was the deal. We offered Jimmy Stewart to John. John took us up on it." Stewart and his agent get furious and storm out of the office.

To this day I have no idea what happened next. I don't know if any money went to the Air Force Academy or not. I do know that our publicity director, Les Kaufman, made the mistake of putting a blurb in the trades saying that Jimmy Stewart was set to star in a show we were going to do called *Family Affair*. Jimmy Stewart immediately calls Don Fedderson demanding a retraction.

"You retract that story and retract it right away. In no way do I want anything to do with Don Fedderson Productions."

Some time later, after leaving Fedderson, I was up for a job as production manager on a show Stewart was starring in. I didn't get the job.

Working on *My Three Sons* was definitely one of the most enjoyable experiences of my career. Sometimes I'm asked, "What's the toughest show you ever did?" No hesitation: *Family Affair*.

MY TOUGHEST SHOW: *FAMILY AFFAIR*

Family Affair was a parlor, bedroom, and bath show. An uncle and his butler take in three children after their parents are killed in an accident. The parents are the uncle's sister and brother-in-law. It was another Fedderson plot with two men running a household. Brian Keith played Uncle Bill, and Sebastian Cabot had the role of the butler, Mr. French. Anissa Jones and Johnnie Whitaker played the two younger kids, Buffy and Jody, and Kathy Garver was their teenage sister, Cissy. There was no action, just dialogue and pretty sets. The show aired from 1966 through 1971.

My typical day on *Family Affair* would go like this. My home phone rings at four in the morning. It's Paula Jones, Anissa's mother.

"Anissa is sick today and can't come in."

I quickly get to the office and at around 5:30 a.m. another call comes in. I know who it is. I pick up the receiver.

"John, John Whitaker here. Johnnie has an upset stomach and can't work today." I'm not surprised; the two of them always seemed to act in tandem. We scramble around, changing scenes and schedules, etc.

We shot the show the same way we did *My Three Sons* except that Brian Keith worked seventy-five days, which gave us a little more latitude. We also had three adults, Brian Keith, Sebastian Cabot and Kathy Garver—that is, if you want to call Brian or Sebastian adults.

My day continues. Brian comes in at 8:00 a.m. for a 7:30 a.m. call. Then he disappears. I get a call from the set.

"Have you seen Brian?"

"Sure, isn't he in makeup?"

"No. Where's Sebastian?"

"His car's in his parking spot."

"Well, he's not on the set, either."

I call Sebastian in his dressing room. "Why aren't you on the set?"

"I'll go on the set when Brian arrives on the set and not before."

I know where Brian is. He went to AA meetings down the street from the studio. I go and bring Brian back to the set. Eight o'clock shooting meant we'd start shooting at nine or nine-thirty. We're in the middle of a shot, and Brian says, "Ya know, I don't think I feel too good, I'm gonna go home."

Then Sebastian says, "I don't feel good either, I think I have to go home, too."

We're left with Kathy Garver, who played the older sister. Kathy really knocked herself out. She was always there on time. She seldom, if ever, got sick.

I get home about 6:30 p.m. Kathy is on the phone. "John, I've got a splinter in my ass."

"What should I do?"

"Just letting you know."

At 11:00 p.m. the phone rings again. It's Sebastian Cabot. "Dear boy, can you hear the ambulance driving away? The paramedics were here; the doctor thought I'd had a mild heart attack. By the way, what time is my call tomorrow?"

"Eight o'clock."

"Well, you know I've had this heart problem."

"I'll tell you what, Sebastian, let's change your call to 9:00 a.m. See you at nine."

And so went my typical day.

My first encounter with Brian Keith was on the Disney lot. I'm visiting my best friend, Joe McEveety, who is doing a show with Brian. Brian is sitting in his makeup chair and when Joe introduces us, Brian mumbles something totally unintelligible. I don't think he remembered seeing me; in fact, in those days I don't think he remembered seeing anybody.

Some time later, Joe McEveety and his wife, Rosemary, are at our house for dinner one night, and the phone rings. The call is for Joe, from the assistant director on the Disney set, telling him he has to get up to Canada right away. Brian had taken Brandon deWilde up there on a drunken spree. "Joe, you're the only one who can get them back."

I wasn't really looking forward to working with Brian.

A couple of days before the first *Family Affair* rehearsal, Brian calls me and gives me a list of demands. I agree to all of them.

"By the way, I want you to be fuckin' sure that that parking space of mine is right across from the stage. I've had trouble before with other people parking in my spot, and it better be empty when I get there, or you're going to fucking well hear from me!"

I'm out there the first morning of rehearsal at 6:00 a.m. making sure no one parks in Brian's space. All of a sudden I'm called in to the stage to see the director. You guessed it. I'm in there for ten minutes, and Brian comes storming onto the stage.

"You fuckin' asshole, I told you, dammit, that my space better be empty, and there's somebody's car in it, and what the hell !#@&*%!"

That was the start of my first day with Brian Keith. Brian's use of the F-word and other words like that were to Brian the same as saying, "Hi, how are you?"

He was very laconic on *Family Affair*. "Ya know I've done all these shows I was proud of—*The Westerner*, directed by Sam Peckinpah, [dropped after thirteen shows], *The Crusader*, and a number of live shows in New York. All of them got critical acclaim, and here I'm doing this piece of shit, and it's a success. I can't believe it!"

Brian was married to Judy Landon, who, in her mind, was a prominent socialite. When Brian would come in to work dragging his tux, I knew that his mood would not be the greatest. It was going to be a night at the opera.

On *Family Affair*, Brian did one take. Good or bad, no second take. If he didn't like a guest star, and we had a lot of guest stars on *Family Affair*, the guest star certainly found out about it very, very quickly.

I have to say that after all the stories you hear about people, you can only judge them by your own experiences with them. In spite of his erratic behavior, I liked Brian. As it turned out, he was very good to me.

The reason *Family Affair* was a success was probably due to Brian's attitude toward the kids. He was different from the typical father figure in a sitcom. He was great with the kids; he loved them, was warm toward them, and didn't get upset if they missed lines. But his language was so bad! The social worker on the set was always begging us to get him to clean up his act. Unfortunately, there wasn't anything that we could do. That was Brian.

Some mornings he'd call my office around 6:00 a.m. Before I could say a word, he'd start this tirade, blasting in my ear, using every cuss word I'd ever heard of and some I'd never heard before.

"Brian, why are you calling me about this?"

"Because you're the only fucking person that's in now!"

Brian only got paid $125,000 a year, for five years. Don Fedderson, at the end of the fourth season, wanted to renegotiate with him and double his salary to $250,000 for the fifth year, with an option for $350,000 for two more years. Brian, in his own inimitable way, said no. This is how Brian was: "I signed for $125,000. That's all I want, and that's all I'm gonna take." He did own twenty-five percent of the show, and he made a ton of money on this deal.

The weirdest situation with Brian was with wardrobe. He only wanted to wear a tattered blue bathrobe on the set. He'd come in wearing a T-shirt and jeans, put on the blue bathrobe and go sit on the set, and then do almost every scene with the blue bathrobe. One day I get a call from the set: "John, Brian won't wear a suit, Brian won't wear a coat, Brian is just sitting in the blue bathrobe."

I go down to the stage. "Brian, do you realize that in this scene you have a line coming up where you say 'Okay kids, see you later, I'm out for the night'? Are you going to take your date out in the blue bathrobe?"

He walks off grumbling, cursing, mumbling, but he does put on a suit.

In another episode, Uncle Bill has supposedly just come back from Terre Haute, Indiana. During the filming, Brian keeps pronouncing the town's name "Terra Hut." We try to get him to pronounce the name correctly. He'll have nothing to do with that. "I'll call it Terra Hut whether you like it or not."

After the show airs, we receive a number of letters from Terre Haute, complaining about Brian's pronunciation. We show him the letters, and he just says, "What the fuck do they know?"

"They live there!"

"Ah, screw 'em."

Brian would do features during his time off. One time when I'm commenting on his schedule, he says, "You know something, John, some day when I'm lying back on my island, a multimillionaire, I'll think, 'John Stephens really helped me along . . . . I wonder what the poor son-of-a-bitch is doing now?'"

Brian was rehearsing once for a Disney film on the *Family Affair* set. He had to play a Western character. Every time I'd walk onto the stage, I'd hear this weird sound and the next thing I knew, I'd be lassoed. He thought this was very funny. My neck didn't.

We had a publicist at Don Fedderson Productions, Les Kaufman. Brian didn't like him. What else was new? For the final two years of the show, Brian put me in a spot, saying, "Any publicity you want, go through John Stephens and if John Stephens says I'll do it, I'll do it. Otherwise fuck off!" (He told me to say "no" to everything.)

The other people in the show would do anything. Sebastian Cabot would open a shoe store if he could get a free pair of shoes.

SEBASTIAN CABOT AND TRAILER SIZES

*S*ebastian Cabot was quite a story. He was not our first choice for Mr. French. Terry Thomas, the gap-toothed Englishman, was. We fly Terry over from England and meet in Don Fedderson's office.

"Well, Terry, what do you think of playing Mr. French?"

"I hate kids! Bathe them? I'd drown the little buggers."

We went with Sebastian.

I found that anybody I ever worked with who had worked for Revue Productions, which later became Universal, automatically had a chip on their shoulder. Revue would promise people various things. They'd never get any of them. Unfortunately both Brian and Sebastian had worked at Revue.

When I first met Sebastian Cabot he asked for the world. He was totally and completely paranoid. We had two trailers, one for Brian and one for Sebastian, exactly the same size. "Why is Brian's trailer larger than mine?"

I explain that it's the same size, and he argues with me, so I get someone to come down with a tape measure and measure his trailer, then go to Brian's and measure his. "They are exactly the same size."

"Well, his looks bigger."

More Sebastian: "John, I'm tired of being the second banana on this show. It isn't right. Look at this script—'two shot favoring Uncle Bill,' 'zoom in on Uncle Bill,' 'extreme close-up, Bill.' I'm really tired of this. Why doesn't it ever say 'two shot favoring Mr. French'?"

"Brian is the star of the show, but I'll look into the matter."

I go to Ed Hartmann and tell him about this. He just looks at me incredulously. I suggest we prepare a script showing everything favoring Mr. French.

Ed Hartmann does a script. The script reads "two shot favoring Mr. French," "extreme close-up of Mr. French," "cut to Mr. French," and on and on. Of course I don't know how Sebastian didn't realize that it wouldn't come out that way in the editing. But it made him happy and got him off my back for the time being.

Sebastian was a very large man, weightwise, and had all kinds of things wrong with him healthwise. The Cabots, Sebastian and his wife Kay, invited my wife Joan and me over for dinner one night. It's the only time we ever left a dinner table starving, and Joan and I were not big eaters. The meal was sparse, and neither of us dared to ask for seconds. We were offered one drink before dinner, then ushered in for the meal, offered a little piece of meat, a tiny piece of a potato, no salad, no bread, and a cup of coffee for dessert. When we left their home, we actually stopped at DuPar's to eat dinner; we were that hungry.

At the studio, Sebastian would go to the commissary every day, get his lunch, and then talk to whomever was at his table, with this huge plate of food in front of him, for forty minutes of the lunch hour. He'd notice the time and say, "Oh my," and in four bites he'd finish the whole lunch.

Anissa Jones, who played Buffy, was really a tragedy in the making. From day one she never wanted to be on the set. Her mother, the mother of all stage mothers, forced her into it. Anissa had to carry that Mrs. Beasley doll around, playing an eight-year-old when she was twelve years old. She had no friends.

Anissa would work five days a week. At 5:00 p.m. on Friday, Les Kaufman, our publicity director, would be at the set with a limo to whisk Anissa and Johnnie Whitaker to the airport. Sometimes it was Anissa alone. Off they'd go to St. Louis to open up a shoe store on Saturday. Then on to Texas to open up something else. On Sunday, Anissa would appear in a parade. Then she'd fly home on Sunday night. She'd learn her lines driving to work on Monday morning. This went on every single week. She hated all of it.

Whether she could act or not, I can't say. She only was allowed to play that singsong little Buffy. The public loved her. No one ever got to know her as a twelve-year-old. I remember I was working on *How the West Was Won* in Kanab, Utah, when my wife called me late one night to tell me that Anissa had overdosed on a combination of drugs, an apparent suicide. I was very upset, but I wasn't surprised. It was a tragedy waiting to happen. Sadly, her brother Paul also overdosed on drugs eight years later.

During the time I worked at Fedderson, this was the only situation where a parent was allowed to control a child. We could do nothing. On *My Three Sons*, all the kids had great parents. We made sure they got their time to play. They never went on too many out-of-town trips to plug the show or anything else. On *Family Affair*, when we tried to talk Don out of this horrendous schedule for the kids, Don said things like "This is what's really helping the show" and "Everybody in America loves Anissa." What Don wanted was another Shirley Temple. I guess at the time the public was ready for another Shirley Temple. Unfortunately Anissa wasn't ready to be Shirley Temple.

I didn't get to know Johnnie Whitaker at all. He seemed to be okay, although he had a very controlling father. He did everything he was told to do. He would take his cue from Anissa. If Anissa was sick, he was sick. He wasn't a problem on the set, and in fact I think he loved being there. He loved the adulation and the rest of what went with it. He went on to act in a few other things, then eventually got out of the business.

Kathy Garver was our workhorse on the show. She was a fine actress and was able to handle anything thrown at her. She knew when we couldn't shoot anything or anyone else that she'd have to learn and rattle off ten and twelve pages of scenes. On one occasion the strain proved too much for her. She wound up having a nervous breakdown from the pressure. Don Fedderson was lucky, as usual. This happened on a Friday, and she was back to work on Monday. During the time Kathy was of an age to date. She started dating Gregg Fedderson, Don's son. Don didn't like this. Gradually Kathy's part on the show became smaller and smaller. She then broke up with Gregg. All of a sudden her parts started to get larger again. Kathy is still in the business and is doing very well, doing voice-overs for cartoons and animated features. She also does acting parts.

And then there were the guest stars . . .

ANN SOTHERN, ETHEL MERMAN, AND ZSA ZSA

*A*nn Sothern was a guest star on *Family Affair*. We had quite a time with her. She comes on the set the first day to check things out. She asks where her dressing room will be.

"Right outside the stage."

"Oh, no, it has to be *on* the stage."

We have the trailer moved inside.

"Just a minute, I'm sure that the toilet and sink hookup will work, won't they, John?"

"Miss Sothern, would you look at the floor please. It's cement. It would be difficult to drill through the cement, add pipes, and hook up your toilet and sink. I hope you understand."

We take the trailer back outside.

The first day of filming she comes up to me. "John, no one has checked with me regarding my lipsticks and makeup." She's trying to get me to put another makeup man on. I don't want to.

I ask her to give me a list of the lipstick colors that she wants. "I'll have someone pick them up for you."

I go upstairs and hand the list to a driver, Marvin Bernard. "Marvin, go to Frends [a well-known theatrical makeup place] and get these lipsticks and makeup." I assume he knows where Frends is.

He doesn't. Instead he goes across the street to a Thrifty Drug Store. I get a call to come down to the set about an hour later. Marvin is standing there, looking chagrined. Miss Sothern appears to be a little upset, to put it mildly.

"John, do you think the driver is going to understand these lipstick shades? And what is this, from Thrifty Drug Store? I asked you to get them from Sig Frends."

Marvin pipes up, "I didn't know what Frends was so I went to Thrifty Drug."

"This isn't right."

"Okay, you win. I'll bring in another makeup person."

Another guest star was Ethel Merman. She shows up the first day of rehearsal to go shopping for her wardrobe.

"John, nice to meet you. Where's the driver and the wardrobe woman that will go shopping with me? By the way, I'll only go to Saks Fifth Avenue. I won't go anywhere else. Did I hear someone say something about Orbachs? I wouldn't go there."

"Miss Merman, we have a deal with Orbachs, not with Saks."

"Fuck your deal! We go to Saks Fifth Avenue, or I'll go back to New York."

"We paid for round-trip tickets from New York for you."

"We'll see, I'll call Mr. Fedderson on this."

She did. That night she was on her way back to New York.

Another famous guest star who worked on both *My Three Sons* and *Family Affair* was Zsa Zsa Gabor. My first encounter with her was actually before those two shows. Fedderson was doing a pilot in New York, *The Charlie Weaver Show,* with Cliff Arquette. They wanted me to cast Zsa Zsa Gabor from Los Angeles. This was the first experience I had with Zsa Zsa.

"Darling, this is what I want. I want you to find my old fencing master. I haven't seen in him about ten years. I can't remember his name. He lives in New York."

Luckily, with the help of contacts, I was able to find him. One thing I don't think many people know about Zsa Zsa is her athletic ability. She was a very accomplished fencer and swam a mile every day. Everything else you've heard about her is true—and then some. I learned a lot from her.

Zsa Zsa decides to tell me about the accommodations she wants in New York. "Also, I'm taking my poodle on board the plane."

Of course, the airline tells me she can't take the poodle. When I give Zsa Zsa the news, she replies, "I'm taking the poodle. Also, John, I want to sit in 3A."

I call the airline and find that seat 3A is taken. I tell Zsa Zsa.

"I'll be in 3A with my dog! Oh, and John, I also want a limousine to pick me up, and it had better be the best one you can get."

The Chrysler Town Car which comes to pick her up was one of the most expensive limos there was. Zsa Zsa doesn't like it. She calls me at home. "This limousine is not appropriate."

"Zsa Zsa, it's the most expensive limo around."

"All right, I'll trust you."

She arrived at the airport, got on the plane with her dog, and was seated in seat 3A. She went to New York. She did the show, and I sort of forgot the whole thing.

My next dealings with Zsa Zsa were on *My Three Sons*. I tell Fred MacMurray that we have Zsa Zsa as a guest star. He's a little bit apprehensive.

"Fred, with Zsa Zsa the only problem is getting her on the set."

She remembered my face from the show in New York, but she never remembered my name. She knew there was a John Stephens at Don Fedderson, and she knew there was a John Stephens she was talking to about her schedule, wardrobe, etc., but she never realized it was the same person.

She calls me about three times to change the dates. I do this.

Zsa Zsa coos, "Oh, you're such a nice man."

Meanwhile, we have our wardrobe people, hairdressers, and makeup people going up to her house. She asks for all kinds of things. When she's told they can't be done, she asks, "Why not?"

"Because John Stephens won't allow them."

"He must be a horrible man."

Another phone call from Zsa Zsa. "John, would you please talk to John Stephens about that other John Stephens?"

I agree to do so.

She calls me the day before we're going to film to give me a list of makeup items which she must have. I write them all down and tell her I'll get them for her. She tells me she wants me to get the makeup at Sig Frends (of course) because he knows what she uses. I tell her I can't because it happens that that day is a Jewish High Holiday, and the store will be closed. She says to just call and tell Sig it's for Zsa Zsa, and he'll open up. I call.

"John, you know I'd do anything for you, but I can't open. It's the High Holiday, I'll be going to temple with my family."

"Could you make an exception? I'll meet you at six o'clock in the morning."

"I can't."

"Sig, you know we buy everything from you on all our shows . . . tell you what, Don Fedderson has a box at Dodger Stadium for all the Dodger games. I'll guarantee the box for you for four games."

"What a dilemma, High Holiday, my son loves baseball . . . all right, I'll do it. I just hope my rabbi doesn't hear about this."

I meet him the next morning at six and get to the studio with all of Zsa Zsa's supplies. She arrives and finds all of the makeup items in her dressing room. Needless to say, she doesn't use a single one of them. They all wind up at her house.

At the end of filming that episode, Zsa Zsa comes up to me. "John, we have a terrible problem. My diamond ring is missing from my dressing room. I know you're insured. I want to be reimbursed for the ring."

"I didn't notice any diamond ring on your finger when you came in. Does anyone else recall seeing it?"

She demands $10,000. We settle for $1,500.

The next time I work with her is on *Family Affair*. This time I figure I'll outsmart her. When she comes onto the set, I'm waiting for her with a guard. "Zsa Zsa, this is your personal guard, Mike. He will be with you at all times and make sure nothing is stolen."

She didn't like that very much.

After Don Fedderson and his wife, Tido, divorced, Zsa Zsa calls Fred De Cordova, who was a friend of hers (and our director). She tells him she would like to meet Don Fedderson and asks if he can arrange it. He says he knows someone who can. He phones me.

"I'm not in that field, Fred."

Zsa Zsa calls me. "John, couldn't you please introduce me?"

"No, Zsa Zsa, I don't do that."

Zsa Zsa never takes no for an answer!

In the fifteen years I worked for Don Fedderson, I very seldom went to lunch with him. This was one of the days. When we get back to his office, his secretary, Lil Holmes says, "Mr. Fedderson, there are some calls that came in while you were at lunch." She rattles them off and closes with,

"Oh, and Zsa Zsa Gabor called saying she was returning your call."

"Zsa Zsa Gabor? I never called her."

HENRY FONDA AND RON HOWARD: BULLETS AND BROWNIES

*N*ot all of the shows we made at Don Fedderson got the kind of ratings that *My Three Sons* and *Family Affair* did. Henry Fonda starred in one of our "disaster shows," *The Smith Family*, which ran for just two seasons, 1970 and 1971. We had several disasters, and *The Smith Family* was one of the biggest. The cast was Henry Fonda, Janet Blair, Ron Howard, Darleen Carr, and Michael-James Wixted. Don Fedderson asks Henry Fonda, "If I can get a deal without a pilot, will you do a TV show?"

"I've only done one show, and it didn't go too well. But I've heard about you, and I'm on board."

Don goes to ABC with the show. "We'll have Henry Fonda playing a policeman during the day and a husband and father by night."

ABC is impressed. "You have a deal. Thirteen shows now to finish out the season and twenty-six shows the next season." Thirty-nine firm shows on just a few words from Don Fedderson.

This type of show had never been done before and with good reason. It's impossible in twenty-six minutes to combine being a policeman by day and coming home to be a husband and father at night. The show would start in with Fonda chasing burglars in the daytime. At night he'd deal with his wife's bake sale, the kid's dance recital, and Ron Howard's basketball game. It didn't work.

The 1970 television season was a truly amazing one. Every star had a show on the air without a pilot. Jim Garner, Tony Curtis, Anthony Quinn, Jimmy Stewart, and Shirley MacLaine. Every one of them bombed.

Henry Fonda was a strange man. I had seen him in many movies. He was a great actor. I'd heard certain things about him. My mother told me she read the book about Fonda in the Broadway play, *Two for the Seesaw*. The people who wrote the play said he was a terrible problem. I told her I'd wait and see for myself.

My first encounter with Fonda was when I was called up to Fedderson's office. A meeting had been going for quite a while. I arrive, and I can tell it isn't going well. Don introduces me to Fonda.

"Well, what are you going to promise me that you're going to do that you can't do?"

"Nice to meet you. I'll tell you what, come down to my office to discuss the thirty-nine suits that Harry Cherry is going to make to your specification, and we'll schedule a time at your convenience to go for a fitting."

"I'll believe that when I see it."

Here's where my gambling surfaced again—I had never called Harry Cherry. I didn't think it would be a problem. It wasn't. Fonda comes down to my office.

"Your appointment with Harry Cherry is tomorrow at 11:00 a.m. Is that good for you?"

"John, you're my man, you get things done. I like that. It's you and me and no one else!"

I had no idea what that was to mean. What it meant was that, like on all of the other shows he did, Fonda picked out one person in the company to join him in going against the rest of the company. I suppose I should have felt lucky but I didn't. It made my job very difficult. His first salvo was to complain about the writer-producer, Ed Hartmann.

"John, keep Ed off the set."

"But Henry—"

"If there are any changes, I'll give them to you."

"Henry, I'm not a writer."

"Don't worry, we'll discuss the changes and then take them to whomever. Just make sure the changes are what we agree on."

Herschel Daugherty was our director. He had directed Fonda in *The Deputy*, Fonda's only other TV show. Herschel was very serious about getting everything right. He was never happy with the way the scripts would come in. He worked and worked and worked. He was the only director I ever worked with who insisted that I come in on Saturdays and meet with him for two hours to go over all of the next week's work. We'd go over the script, the sets, and all the production. While I didn't enjoy it, I agreed to do it. I'd try to get out of there as soon as possible. This entailed taking my dog Scooter with me. Scooter would constantly growl at Herschel. It didn't work. Herschel stuck to his guns and wouldn't let me go. This went on Saturday after Saturday.

Finally we come to a very, very important day in my life, in late November. "Herschel, whatever you want to discuss, I'll stay here till midnight tonight, but I am not coming in tomorrow, no matter what happens. I'm watching the Michigan–Ohio State game and then my son and I are going to the USC–UCLA game. Whatever you do, don't, under any circumstances, call me on Saturday!"

"Okay, fine, fine, I'll do that. I have no questions really. So everything is fine."

"Okay, but remember, no calls tomorrow."

I go home that night all excited about the next day. At halftime of the Michigan–Ohio State game, I go in to shower. My son comes in. "There's a Herschel Daugherty on the phone for you."

"Did you tell him I wasn't home?"

"No."

"Hello. Okay. What do you want, Herschel?"

"John, I hate to bother you, but a big problem came up that I really need you to help me solve. I'm in the studio now. It'll just take you at the most an hour."

"Herschel, I'm not coming in! I'm watching the second half of the game, then I'm going to the USC–UCLA game. I told you I'm not coming in."

"John, this is work. What's more important to you, work or a football game?"

"The football game."

"John, I'm going to call Don Fedderson and tell him that that's the way you feel. This means we're not going to get anything done next week 'cause you want to go to some stupid football game!"

I pause. He laughs.

"Gotcha, didn't I, John?"

Fonda had it in his contract that he wouldn't work with a "scale" actor. He felt that scale actors were just there to say their lines and get out when the scene was over. He needed feedback from the actor he was working with.

"If they're not up to my level, I try to bring them there. They can't respond, so the scene ends up making me look like I'm chewing up the scenery. I won't do that. I don't care about meeting the actors, but I definitely want to know they aren't scale actors." On *The Smith Family* I got called down to the set more times to be told to fire some actor that the star didn't like than on any other show I ever worked on.

The Smith Family got worse and worse. It was way down in the ratings. At the end of the first season, Fonda calls me down to the set.

"Listen, there are going to be a lot of changes for the second season. First of all, Ed Hartmann will no longer be the writer-producer; you are going to produce the show. Secondly, Janet Blair is going to be gone. Thirdly, Michael-James Wixted is English. He has a heavy English accent. What kind of family is this? My wife's from New York, my oldest son is from North Hollywood, my daughter is from San Francisco, my youngest is from England, and I'm from Nebraska. I want Herschel Daugherty to remain as director. Call a meeting with Fedderson. We'll get this straightened out."

Two weeks later we have the meeting—Don Fedderson, Fred Henry, Henry Fonda, and myself. Fonda presents his demands to Fedderson in a very harsh manner. Fedderson pushes a button on the intercom. "Miss Holmes, will you please bring in Mr. Fonda's contract."

Miss Holmes brings in the contract; Don looks it over.

"Everything seems to be in order. Here you are, Hank. I don't need this, and I don't need you."

Fonda blanches. "Don, maybe I've been a bit hasty. Let me think about this."

"Fine, take the contract. I'll give you a week to think about it, but I'm not going to approve a single thing you asked for."

We started season two on schedule with every single person, cast and crew, exactly the same as before. This is the way it used to be in Hollywood.

Everything that's ever been said about Ron Howard is right on! He's not only a good actor, he's a good person. The only thing I dreaded about Ron finally happened. Larry King was interviewing him on King's TV show.

"Ron, you've had so many successes in your life; you never did have a failure, did you?" I'm listening to this and thinking, "Don't say it Ron, please don't say it."

"Yeah, Larry, I had one, *The Smith Family.*"

"Tell us about it." (No, no, don't say anything . . .)

Ron goes on and on about the show and how he was teased about its theme song, "Primrose Lane," which hardly fit a detective show. I knew how he felt because I was teased about that too.

One day Ron told me he was entering the Kodak's Amateur Directors Contest. He was sixteen years old at the time. He asked me if I could get permission for him to use the backlot to film. I called Bob Norvet at CBS and set it up for him. He shot the film. He showed it to me when it was done. It was absolutely sensational. He finished second in the contest. That was the first show Ron ever directed.

A number of years later when I was doing *How the West Was Won* at MGM, there was a fellow called Howard who was the program and practices person at ABC. Every time he called me, I'd go crazy. It was always, "You can't do this" and so on. Sally Hope, my assistant, buzzes me on the intercom. "I didn't catch the first name, but Mr. Howard's on line one."

"Oh no, not again." I pick up the phone. "Hi there."

"Hi, John, this is Ron Howard, I don't know if you remember me . . . "

Here's Ron Howard. He's done all these big features, and he's asking me if I remember him.

JOHN FORSYTHE AND WALTER BRENNAN IN ROME

To Rome with Love, starring John Forsythe and Walter Brennan, aired during the 1969 and 1970 seasons. This show was a complete disaster. It was basically *My Three Sons* with three girls instead of three boys, and with the location moved from Bryant Park to Rome. John Forsythe was a newspaper reporter, and Walter Brennan was his crusty grandfather. Sound familiar? Fred MacMurray was always complaining that we were simply recycling *My Three Sons* scripts. No comment from me.

Working on *To Rome with Love* was the only time I ever encountered politics on a set. John Forsythe was an extreme liberal. Walter Brennan thought John Wayne was a Communist! I remember being at Brennan's house in Moorpark. Walter showed me his bunker. He was positive the Russians were going to invade the United States. He had firearms and a two-year supply of food. I had never seen anything like it before, and I haven't since.

By the time *To Rome with Love* was in production, Walter was getting on in years. He had emphysema. In addition to this, he could not and did not want to learn his lines. We hired Barney McNulty to write Walter's lines on these large cards and then hold them up so he could read his dialogue during each scene. The problem was, he'd never be looking at the children when he spoke. He'd be looking at the cue cards. This made it difficult for the girls.

John Forsythe was a very well-respected actor. Everyone liked John. He was a total professional. John heard that Brian Keith was working on the lot. "John, could Brian come see me?"

"Sure, John, I'll take care of it."

I go find Brian. "Brian, John Forsythe knows you're working here and wishes you'd come by and say hello. He remembers you from New York."

"Fuck him!"

I talk Brian into going. John greets him warmly. "Brian, Brian, how are you, how've you been?"

"Fine. I can't fucking believe you're still working."

Things get worse on the set. I call John and Walter into my office. I feel like a principal of a grammar school.

"Guys, I'm sick and tired of you both handing out flyers, tacking up signs on stage doors, and giving political speeches. This has to stop.

I don't want anybody discussing politics on the set or attempting to influence the crew or the cast one way or the other on how to vote. It's not what we're here for. We're here to make a TV show, not to try to run the politics of the country."

Walter had lots of Hollywood stories. Here's one he liked to tell.

In the old days the most feared men in Hollywood were the studio gate guards. There was a guard working at Selznick Studios. Walter drove in. The guard stopped him.

"Do you have a pass to drive on?"

"My name's on the list, I'm sure."

"What's your name?"

That is the worst thing you can say to anybody, especially to someone who had won three Academy Awards.

"My name is Walter Brennan. If Mr. Selznick asks where I am, tell him I'm at the beach."

"Okay, I'll do that. Which beach?"

"Just the beach."

We did a number of pilots at Don Fedderson. One of the early pilots was with Jack Lord. Jack and I had worked together on *The Millionaire*. The name of this pilot was *The Quiet Man*. It was a Western that had nothing to do with the John Wayne movie of the same name.

Jack Lord was the first method actor I'd ever encountered. The first scene we film entails Jack running into a dry goods store and giving Wanda Hendrix some good news. Everybody is standing around. Jack comes up to me.

"Look, I'm going to be running up and down. I'll be yelling certain things. When I'm ready I'll point my finger, you nudge the director, and he can say 'Action!'"

Jack starts running in place, saying, "Happy, happy, happy, happy."

The crew doesn't know what's going on, nor does the director.

"Happy, happy, happy, happy."

Jack points at me; I nudge the director; the director says, "Roll 'em."

Jack roars into the store and gives Wanda Hendrix the good news. It doesn't work on the first two takes because of the background noise. The crew has no idea what's going on.

The sponsors weren't as "happy" as Jack was. The show was never sold.

LUNCH WITH RAY WALSTON—I MAKE A FEW MISTAKES

$\mathcal{O}$ne of the funnier shows we did at Fedderson was a pilot, *Satan's Waitin'*, which we shot in 1967. It wasn't meant to be funny. The star was Ray Walston. He played the devil. The guest star was Jo Van Fleet, who had won an Academy Award for *East of Eden*. Don was the executive producer, and he brought in two writer-producers, Joel Malone and Tommy Tomlinson. They were very well-known radio writers. I don't know if they'd done any TV shows. I know they had never produced one. Tommy was a very nice fellow, but Joel was off in another world. We hired the best cameraman in Hollywood, Jimmy Wong Howe.

During the production of this pilot Don Fedderson and Fred Henry were both out of the country. This put me in charge. We start the first day of rehearsal. Charles Haas is the director. He is an elderly gentleman who has done a lot of television. We start in on the reading. At page three, Charles addresses the cast. "I'm sorry this company's too cheap to hire the man to play this part, so therefore I'll read it."

Ray Walston blanches. "Just a minute, I'm Satan, I do all of these parts."

Everything went downhill from there. The director didn't understand the script. This did not sit too well with the cast.

After three days of filming, I realize we have another disaster on our hands. I decide to save all the money I can.

I tell James Wong Howe a little white lie. "Jim, we have to go faster. This pilot is presold." (In those days this was a commonly used term.) It wasn't true. It never was.

People don't realize that Jimmy did *Picnic* in eighty days. Then he could turn around and shoot a Roger Corman feature in seven days. He could go as fast or slow as the production called for.

"I understand, John. We'll go fast!"

"Jimmy, Jo Van Fleet has just done the master. She's going to go and have a drink. She'll change her makeup, do whatever with her hair.

She won't be back for an hour. Is it possible, even though you're lit in the direction where you'd normally shoot her, to turn around and cover the other people? Then we'll turn around again and probably be waiting for her. You know when this show goes, and it's certain to go, you'll be directing four or five of them." I did not consider that a cardinal sin.

He's ready in fifteen minutes. Lee Phillips was the costar of the show. We're just getting ready to shoot his close-up when onto the stage walks Jo Van Fleet. "What the hell are you doing? I'm ready."

Jimmy looks at me. We immediately relight and are ready in ten minutes. We shoot her close up.

As we're nearing the end of filming, Jo comes up to me. "John, I'm not going to finish this show unless you give me all of the wardrobe that I wore in the show. Besides, Joel Malone promised it to me."

"If that's what Joel told you, then you've got it."

While we're on the last scene, I get hold of the wardrobe man. "Get all of Jo Van Fleet's wardrobe out of her dressing room. Lock it up, turn off the lights, and leave."

She did keep the last outfit she had on when the show finished.

There was one truly funny incident on *Satan's Waitin'*. We break for lunch, and Ray Walston and I walk over to the commissary to eat. Now, Ray Walston, as any of you who are old-time NFL football fans will remember, was the name of the famous Philadelphia Eagles's receiver. At this time the Pro Bowl was being held in Los Angeles. As Ray and I walk into the commissary, Bill Frawley spots me from his table and calls out, "Hey John, join us for lunch."

Ray and I go over to sit with Bill and without even thinking, I introduce them.

"Ray, this is Bill Frawley; Bill, this is Ray Walston."

"What, you're Ray Walston? You're a little guy."

Now Ray, who has no idea there's another Ray Walston, says gruffly, "Whaddaya mean I'm a little guy!"

"You're a little guy for a football player."

"I'm not a football player, I'm an actor!"

"Oh."

Another failure we made in 1967 was *Tramp Ship* starring Neville Brand and Mike Minor, Don Fedderson's son. We needed to find a location at a pier that was totally uninhabited and would be available for one day of filming. We planned on starting around 6:00 a.m. on one morning and finishing around 4:00 a.m. the next.

I drive down to the harbor, looking for a good location. I find a great spot. No ships around. It's totally deserted. I get out of the car and see this guy sitting on the dock eating his lunch. He's wearing a hard hat and has a tool belt on. I explain about the TV pilot and that we want to use the pier for one day.

"You say you want to film on the nineteenth? This pier is going to be torn down at 10:00 a.m. on the twentieth."

"That would be great. We'll be out of here by then. I tell you what, I'll give you $100 now and $100 when we get down here with our equipment, to make sure everything is intact. That's $200 free and clear."

"Fine."

He takes the $100.

We get down to the pier on the nineteenth and get all of our material we need done before boarding the ship and heading out to sea. We get back that afternoon about four o'clock. We shoot until three-thirty the next morning. We have rain effects, storms, big fights, the whole kit and caboodle. When we finally finish, we go to the bar, which has been kept open for us, for a few drinks.

The plan is to rest up for a couple of hours and then go back to the studio. Don Fedderson comes up to me about thirty minutes later. I've had a couple of drinks by then, as has Sid Sidman, the AD.

"You know something, kid, I'm not really happy with the way Mike's song went at sea. I want to go out there tomorrow and redo Mike's song. It's going to be better, and this is really the thrust of the show." (I'm thinking to myself, is this a musical?)

You never say no to Don. I have to try to find the guy to whom I had given the $200 and find out if we can get whatever company he works for not to tear down the pier until the next day. I have no card, and no name. I can only hope he'll show up by 6:00 a.m. Luckily, he does. I tell him my problem.

"You do have a problem."

"Can't you call your boss and explain the situation? It'll only be one more day. I can make it worth your while in cash."

"No, I can't reach him. He's on another job, and I won't be able to get in touch with him in time. I tell you what, give me $5,000 cash.

I'll split it with my crew. We'll stall the demolition. But only for one day."

No time to argue. "Deal."

We always have access to cash, so it's not a problem. I give the money to the guy and ask for a receipt. He says he doesn't want to sign anything because he and his crew are doing this unknown to the boss. I'm in a hurry. We have to get started because of the time limit. I thank him and go off to the ship. We finish Mike's song. We're out in plenty of time.

About a week later, I find myself down in the same area looking for another location. I notice that the pier is still standing, and there are a couple of fishing boats nearby. I go into a nearby café to have a cup of coffee. All of sudden I look up. There's my hard-hat friend.

"I see the pier is still up. What happened?"

"Well, I got another job, and we had to delay this one for ninety days."

"What did your boss say?"

"I am the boss."

Five thousand two hundred dollars down the drain.

TWENTY-FIVE GIRLS WITH BEAUTIFUL *WHATS?*

The Fedderson Company decided to start their own commercial division. Don brought in his brother-in-law, Jack Minor, and a fellow by the name of Peck Prior to run the company. Because Jack and Peck knew me, they said it was important that I get involved. I'd never done a commercial in my life.

Nobody told me that commercials were different from TV. When producing a TV show, the most important thing is to have all the equipment ready, be on the set at the scheduled time, and be prepared to start shooting. Commercials don't work that way. Commercials are take after take, after take, after take. What I didn't know was that although it was good to have everything ready, it didn't really matter. We couldn't start shooting until the sponsors and the advertising people arrived. If the schedule said 8:00 a.m., and they didn't arrive until 9:30 a.m., we would have to wait. On top of that, many times when they did arrive, they'd see the shot that we had planned and have a meeting about it. Then they'd call their Chicago office to get the go-ahead on the shot. The shot was always changed. I wasn't used to this, nor was the crew that I hired. We were used to just setting up, shooting, setting up, and shooting, bang, bang. All of a sudden it was slow and slower.

The commercial I remember the most clearly was for Schmidt's Beer. Everyone thought we were doing a commercial for Schlitz Beer. "Uh-uh, Schmidt's Beer out of Carling, Pennsylvania."

This was a classic. The producer-director from the advertising agency comes out to Los Angeles. He's looking for a New York setting. "Why didn't you stay in New York?"

"I'm divorcing my wife, and I can get a quick divorce in Mexico." Great reason.

We scout all over looking for locations that can pass for New York. We finally pick some that meet with his approval. He tells me the next step is for the ad agency people to approve them.

"But I thought you—"

"No, no, they have the final word."

The next day the people from the ad agency arrive. They don't approve of any of the locations. We pick out new ones, which they agree to. We're ready to start filming in two days. (Ha, ha.) Then the ad agency people tell me the locations have to be approved by the clients, Schmidt's Beer. The clients arrive. I don't have to tell you what happens. They don't approve of any of the locations. We pick out new ones. *Finally* we're ready to go. What should have taken a couple of days has now taken a couple of weeks.

After the first day's dailies, the clients decide we need to reshoot. "We don't like the looks of the neighbors coming out to greet the stars of the commercial." We had seen at least forty couples to cast that scene. "Look at them, would you want people like that living next door to you? I don't like them. Get new people and we'll reshoot the scene."

The clients also impress upon me that the most important thing in the commercial is the beer pouring. It's an art. They ask me if the cameraman, Stanley Cortez, has ever done any beer-pouring shots.

"Guys, Stanley Cortez was Orson Welles's cameraman. He shot *The Magnificent Ambersons*, *The Night of the Hunter*, and many other big features. He's a two-time Academy Award nominee. He's a brilliant cameraman."

"So what? Has he ever shot a beer-pouring shot?"

"Those are inserts."

"No. This is the essence of the commercial!"

They're right. I manage to convince them to keep Stanley. Next they tell me that the prop master is the other key man on a beer commercial. He has to be the one who, offscreen, pours the beer perfectly. "There's an art to pouring beer."

"Carl Nugent is our prop master. He's done many big features at MGM—*The Wizard of Oz, Green Dolphin Street,* and *The Postman Always Rings Twice.*"

"Has he ever done beer-pouring shots?"

I won't repeat what Carl says when I ask him if he has ever done a beer-pouring shot. We keep Carl as prop master, but they bring a specialist in beer pouring out from New York. It takes about nine days to film a sixty-second commercial—six more days than it would take to film a thirty-minute TV episode.

Another commercial I'll always remember involved Kasper, Kapsis & Krone. They were the three admen for a Volkswagen commercial that every other company had turned down. It was impossible to film. The idea was a Volkswagen going around and around in infinity with a blue background. No one knew how to do it without taking literally weeks to shoot. This would make the cost prohibitive. Our Jack Minor said we would do it. "If we do this, the ad agency will give us ten more commercials to do this year." Fat chance.

We attempted to make the Volkswagen commercial. We filmed for about eight days. The other companies were right. It could not be done. (Obviously this was before the advances in computers.) Another lesson learned.

When people talk about the casting couch, kickbacks, money bribes, and things like that—I found these things to be much more prevalent in the commercial field than in any other field I worked in, before or since. The casting couch was simply this. You'd be ready to film a commercial, and all of a sudden all these "product" extras—extras who would physically touch the product, as opposed to the people in the background—would come up saying that so-and-so had told them to report and that they were to be product extras. They would get more money than the background extras. This was especially prevalent during a Chevrolet commercial we did, where the director, who shall remain nameless, was off with one of these "product extras" while we were filming one of the most important scenes of the commercial. There were a number of Chevrolets coming onto the freeway from two different off-ramps and merging together. The next day I'm sitting with the sponsors, ad agency people, and the director. We're watching the dailies. One of the sponsors lets out a scream. He utters some words he must have learned from Brian Keith.

"What fucking son-of-a-bitch let this happen?! There are stop signs on the ramps, and none of the Chevrolets are stopping! How in the hell can we put a commercial like this on the air? Who's responsible for this?"

None of us would answer. We had to reshoot the whole thing. That was the kind of thing that cropped up on our commercials.

The last commercial I ever worked on was for Speidel Watches. Besides being the production manager, I was also the casting director. I was told to bring in twenty-five girls with beautiful wrists by the next day.

"Twenty-five girls with beautiful wrists?! Legs, lips, hair, maybe, but *wrists*?!"

I brought in another casting director and went over to Don's office. "I appreciate the extra money, but I don't think I should be with the commercial company any more."

"You know something, John, the commercial company has told me exactly the same thing."

DON FEDDERSON

*D*on Fedderson. Who was he? He was probably the most unique, successful producer I ever worked for. Don came from Kansas City. He had no background in the entertainment business. As a child, the movie bug bit him. Strangely enough, the bug seemed to have passed away by the time he got into high school. I doubt that he ever saw a movie from the time he was sixteen. He didn't have a lot of money, but fortunately for him he married very well. His wife was Tido Minor, who came from a very wealthy Kansas family. Tido's brother, Jack Minor, was the assistant general manager of the Plymouth Division of the Chrysler Corporation.

Don came out to California and settled in San Francisco. He got a job at a local radio station. He then moved on to Los Angeles and went to work at KLAC-TV (later KCOP) as station manager. He put *Life with Elizabeth*, written and produced by George Tibbles and starring Betty White, on the air. In the meantime, Jack Minor bought *The Lawrence Welk Show* for the Dodge Division of Chrysler. Jack insisted that his brother-in-law oversee the show. Don left KLAC and took *The Liberace Show* and Betty White with him. He formed his own company, Don Fedderson Productions, and brought in Fred Henry as his partner. Fred had been with Don in San Francisco and was the program director at KLAC. Fred handled the business end and Don the creative end of Fedderson Productions.

Don relied entirely on instinct. He never cared what anyone had done before. When he met you, he would look at you and say, "I think this will work." Or "We'll get in touch with you." You always had to meet Fred Henry first. If Fred liked you, Don would hire you.

Don was a rather cold man. While his shows were very warm, Don was not. Apparently he had read how moguls' offices should be. No matter what the weather was outside, Don's office thermostat was always set at sixty degrees. If Don called a meeting in the summertime, we'd have to wear jackets in his office. Lil Holmes, his secretary of many years, would always serve coffee. Not in coffee cups, not in coffee mugs, but in highball glasses. Immediately everyone was ill at ease. Just to get out of there, we'd agree with anything Don wanted, right or wrong.

Don's interest in all of his company's shows was the following: final say on all casting for pilots, approval of the director for the pilot, approval of the script, and approval of all postproduction. He was on the set for every shot of the pilot. Once he sold the show, he would then only concern himself with the postproduction.

Sometimes casting with Don could be difficult. We were doing a pilot called *The Chairman*, and I recommended Phil Ober.

"Who's that?"

"He played Deborah Kerr's husband in *From Here to Eternity*."

"Didn't see it, you'll have to bring him in."

And so it went.

We had a party in Palm Springs for Bill Demarest's eightieth birthday. Don was the master of ceremonies. He introduced the luminaries. He'd never heard of any of them. His best introduction of the evening was "Ladies and gentlemen, I give you one of Hollywood's most famous people, Frank Crappa."

Don Fedderson produced *The Millionaire*, *My Three Sons*, *Family Affair*, *The Smith Family*, *To Rome with Love*, *Liberace*, *The Lawrence Welk Show*, *Who Do You Trust?*, a number of pilots, and movies of the week. Don would personally take the pilots back to Chicago and sell them. In those days, they were bought by the sponsors, not by the networks. If he sold a pilot, he would tell us by telephone how much he had sold it for. We would know exactly how much money we had to make the show.

All of Don's money for the pilots came directly from Bank of America. All of our shows made money. We used the adage: "You shoot the script, not the budget." The scripts were tailored to easily be made within the confines of the budget. We had one set of books. If you owned two-and-a-half percent of a Don Fedderson show, you made money. Although Don was a cold man, he was extremely generous. Every year you'd go up to receive your bonus check. Don would leave the date blank so you could fill in whatever date would suit your tax purposes.

Don's method of casting children seemed bizarre but never failed. He would see several children, narrow the choice down to two or three and then instead of calling the children back, he'd meet their parents. His idea was to keep the kids as young as possible for as long as possible. He did not believe in the children growing up on the show. If the child's parents were tall, the child was not hired. We used to joke about Don having the children sleep in vises to prevent them from getting taller.

Don's only real interest was in the making of a pilot. Once a show sold, he turned everything over to us, the people making the show. Don would read the original stories and scripts and say "yes" or "no" and that was it. He had nothing to do with the casting of the episodes.

Don led a double life. There was his business. No problems with business. There was his family. Lots of problems with family.

He thought his children should have jobs. When his eldest son Mike was eleven, Don told him to get a paper route. Mike dutifully got a paper route.

"Dad, I can't be up at five o'clock in the morning delivering papers by myself. You're going to have to do it with me."

Don would get up at 4:30 a.m. and do all the folding, wrapping, etc. of the papers. Then he'd get Mike up and drive him around delivering the papers. Mike would be asleep in the back seat. Don would be driving up and down the streets of Bel Air, throwing the papers out of the window onto the various lawns. Finally Mike couldn't take sleeping in the back seat any longer.

"Dad, why are we doing this? We're millionaires!"

That was the end of Mike's paper route.

One day I get a phone call from Don, telling me that he has someone he wants me to hire to work under Fred Henry and me. One of his sons, Gregg.

"No, Don. If there's something important to go to the set, it will never get there. Gregg will see some cute girl and take off after her. He hasn't learned responsibility."

"John, is there anything in particular you're basing this on?"

"I'll give you an example. Gregg came to me one day and asked to borrow my car. He wanted to go to lunch off the lot. I let him take the car. Three hours later, he returned."

"Did he come up to your office and explain?"

"No, but that's not the worst part. I was taking Joan out to dinner that evening, and she needed something out of the glove compartment. When she reached in, she found a card for the Body Shop. She said to me, 'John, could you explain this please?' I said, 'Joan, I have no idea what that is, but it looks like a place you would take your car in to get it painted or something. What's the big deal?' And she said, 'Turn it over, as there's a girl's name and phone number on the back.'"

The Body Shop is still one of the most famous strip joints on the Sunset Strip. Don saw my point.

FRED HENRY—BRIAN KEITH TO THE RESCUE

A month later Don calls me into his office. "John, we've got to find a job for Gregg."

This isn't a request, it's an order. I come up with a great idea. (Great for me.)

"Don, I'll get him into the Screen Extras Guild as a stand-in. He can be on the set all day. He'll learn all about production. I think this will be just the thing for him!" Don is very happy.

I call Cesar Sortino, the head of the Screen Extras Guild, and tell him what I want. "John, you want me to take a millionaire's son into the Guild?"

"Cesar, you have my word on this. He'll pay the initial fee and dues. At the most he'll last one month. You'll have the money. He'll be gone, and no one will be put out of work over this. Also for the month, put one of your members on the set who needs the money, and we'll pay him." Cesar agrees to this.

I call Gregg in and tell him about the job. He isn't thrilled about it but says okay. Gregg's first day on the job, I get a call from the assistant director, John Gaudioso. "Gregg is late. He was supposed to be here at 7:30 a.m. It's eight now and no Gregg."

At nine o'clock Greg shows up. Then at ten o'clock I get another phone call. "Gregg wants to see you on the set right away."

I go down to the stage. Gregg greets me. "There's no chair for me."

"Gregg, there are chairs for the director and cast and certain members of the crew, but I've never heard of a stand-in having his own chair. No, Gregg, no chair."

I get another call from John Gaudioso. "John, it's twelve o'clock."

"So?"

"Gregg has gone to lunch. I told him we don't break for lunch until one-thirty. He told me he was leaving because he had something to do. What should I do?"

"Keep filming."

At three-thirty the next call comes in. "Gregg just got back from lunch."

This call follows an hour later. "You can't believe this."

"I can believe anything."

"Gregg just left for the day."

"Sounds like he had a very tough day."

Gaudioso doesn't laugh.

That night I get home, and Joan greets me at the door. "Gregg called at five o'clock and said to tell you he quit."

I call Cesar Sortino at the Guild the next morning. "Cesar, I lied to you by twenty-nine days."

"What do you mean?"

"Gregg lasted one day. Put the money to good use."

All of Don's children seemed to have this M.O. except Mike, whose professional name is Mike Minor. He was a regular on *Petticoat Junction* and has had a good career in soap operas.

The only critical mail we ever got on *My Three Sons* was from parents complaining about the ease with which every issue was resolved. This was a trap that Don fell into when dealing with his family. On our TV shows, all problems were solved in twenty-six minutes. Don's children told me that was the way it was at home. One night a week they would have a family dinner. At this time they would all tell Don their problems. He would solve them in twenty-six minutes. This was the 1960s, and it took a lot more fathering than a twenty-six minute dinner once a week.

I doubt if Don Fedderson Productions would have become as successful as it did without Fred Henry, Don's partner and longtime friend. Fred was a man of few words. He taught me many things and helped me in many ways. He was my mentor and a great man. I admired him deeply.

One day he calls me in to his office.

"Johnny, there's nothing you have that's written down. Is there? It's all in your head?"

"Pretty much."

"What if you're driving home one night and have an accident? No one else will know what's going on here."

That's the way Fred was, terse, to the point, with a rather strong manner. I appreciated that.

He also liked to tease. He says to me one day in his joking manner, "Johnny, you know one of your jobs is to drive Gregg Fedderson back and forth to the sets and things like that. Well, my children might be needing a ride to and from Sunday school on Sundays, so you'd better keep your Sunday mornings free." That was Fred's sense of humor.

Fred was definitely the glue that held the company together. He was a rather shy, quiet man. He would often go down to the set. He'd stay in the background, just listening and watching whatever was going on, never speaking to anyone. I'd get calls asking who the man was that was hanging around the set. I'd explain it was Fred Henry, who really ran the company.

I was becoming leery of the Fedderson company after years of successful shows. I had reached the point in my career when I felt the company was out of touch with reality. Then out of the clear blue sky I get a call from Brian Keith in Hawaii.

"John, you know the show I'm doing, *The Little People*."

"I've heard of it, but I've never seen it."

"Well, they're changing the name to *The Brian Keith Show*, and I told them I'm not doing the show again unless you're the producer, and they fire everybody else."

"GARRY MARSHALL'S ITALIAN, BRIAN"

I can't believe what Brian is saying. "What?!"

"That's it. Do you want to do the show and become a producer?"

"Can I think about it?"

"Yeah, but let me know tomorrow."

I talk it over with my wife, and we both agree it would be a good move. The next day I call him. "Brian, I'd love to do the show."

"Okay, you're hired."

"Don't I have to meet anybody?"

"Maybe, but fuck 'em. You've got the job."

I did have an interview of sorts, with Jerry Leider and Tom Kuhn. It was the most interesting interview I'd ever had. They told me that the network had to approve me. Fine. They went over some of Brian's demands. Some of the demands shocked me. Brian insisted that every single person in the creative area be fired. That included the creator and executive producer, Garry Marshall. In Brian's words, he wasn't funny, and he didn't understand humor. I looked up incredulously. Garry Marshall didn't understand humor?

"Also he wants the director Jerry Thorpe fired. Oh yeah, he wants the whole crew fired too."

I had worked with Jerry Thorpe, and I thought he was a tremendous director. A bigger problem with the firing of Jerry loomed on the horizon. At the time Jerry Thorpe was going with Shelley Fabares, the female star of the show. I figured she wouldn't be too happy about the change. I was right.

I go in to see Garry Marshall. "Hi, John. You know why Brian wants me fired."

"No, I sure don't."

"Brian thinks I'm Jewish and Brian is very anti-Semitic. I'm not Jewish, I'm Italian. I really don't need Brian Keith."

"Garry, that's not true. A lot of people think that about Brian. Actually, Brian is very anti-New York. Anybody from New York, Brian doesn't like." Why? I don't know. I know Brian's father, Robert Keith (Brian's real name was Robert Keith, Jr.), was on Broadway and Brian got his start on Broadway. For some reason he just hated New Yorkers. "Garry, he's seen your license plate, and it says 'Bronx 1.' That's the only reason. Believe me, there's no way I'm going to let Brian fire you, nor would I ever fire you."

What we agreed on was for Garry to be the executive consultant. Brian was the executive producer, and I was the producer. Jerry Thorpe and the rest of Brian's "get rid ofs" were gotten rid of. (I made it official and left Don Fedderson Productions in 1971.)

The Brian Keith Show concerned a pediatrician and his daughter, also a pediatrician, who worked in Hawaii. The show was a minor fiasco. It wasn't that strong to begin with, but with Brian in charge of everything, it went from a mini-fiasco to a full-blown catastrophe. He even insisted on doing the theme song himself, with a bunch of Hawaiian instruments. This didn't help things. Our main audience was in the Midwest, picking up the *Family Affair* viewers Brian had had before. Nobody in Iowa knew or cared about Hawaiian culture.

Brian said, "Fuck 'em, we'll teach 'em."

We would send scripts over to Hawaii and then the phone calls would start.

"That fuckin' script you sent me is no good, I tossed it in the ocean. Send me another one. Are we educating the people or aren't we?"

"No, Brian."

"Then fuck 'em!"

The Brian Keith Show lasted one year.

I PRODUCE TV'S WORST NINETY-MINUTE
MOVIE OF THE WEEK

*W*hen the complete history of television is written, I think my name will be mentioned for having produced possibly the worst ever ninety-minute movie of the week. With regards to the *Wonder Woman* pilot, no one ever starts a TV show with the idea of making something as bad as you can make it, but you can, through a series of unfortunate incidents, manage to come up with something that doesn't work in any way, shape, or form.

I was at Warner Bros. in 1973, nearing the end of my contract, when they asked me if I'd like to do a movie of the week backdoor pilot. They gave me three scripts to read. One was for *Wonder Woman*. I knew the character from comic books. "This is going to be great. Another *Batman*."

I should have figured that something was strange when they got me to sign the contract to produce the pilot without first meeting the executive producer. I finally meet him. He's a very imposing man, to say the least—six feet three, husky, Rasputin-like, with a voice to match. This is John D. F. Black, the executive producer and writer of this epic!

"John, good to meet you. I hope you're excited about this. Gloria Steinem has endorsed it. This will be a serious, true action series, showing women's power and will be one of the greatest pieces ever. There will be no comedy."

It's all I can do to keep a straight face. I keep waiting for him to say he's kidding or something—but he doesn't. I leave his office in shock. How can he be serious? It's so obviously a light, fun-filled project like *Batman* or *Superman*. Who could possibly take this seriously?

I call my wife. "Look, they're paying us a lot of money. He's the executive producer, and writer, so even if it's a disaster—and I'm sure it will be—no one will blame me. When it's over, we'll take the kids on a cruise and forget about it."

Joan agrees, so here we go.

We saw a lot of women for the role of Wonder Woman and finally selected Cathy Lee Crosby, who I thought was absolutely perfect for the role. In the final analysis, even if a young Ingrid Bergman had gotten the part, it wouldn't have come off. It just didn't work in any way. I took exception to the review of the second *Wonder Woman* pilot that was sold, which starred Lynda Carter. The review said that at least here was an athletic woman, when in the first pilot, Cathy Lee Crosby looked like she "just stepped out of a Bergdorf Goodman gown." This was totally untrue. Cathy Lee actually was a track athlete at USC. She did almost all of her own stunts, as opposed to Lynda Carter, who did only a few of her own stunts.

Cathy was faced with problems from the outset—like the script, for example. Her main problem was dealing with John D. F. Black. Just before we started to film, Black called a big meeting with Vince McEveety, Cathy Lee, and myself.

"Cathy, I want to tell you this. From now on I'm in total control of your personal life. I don't want you to have sex with anyone, do drugs with anyone, or smoke with anyone. I want you to live a completely pure life. Just remember, you are Wonder Woman."

What a wonderful way to kick off the show.

The rest of the cast was interesting. I think we could have ruined a future star's career. Lucky for him, we didn't. I saw this blonde fellow in a *Barnaby Jones* show doing one scene. I go into Eddie Foy's office. Eddie's our casting director. I tell him about the actor in *Barnaby Jones*. Eddie says, "Nick Nolte, I know him. He's a good actor. I've tried to sell him here, let's bring him in."

Nick Nolte comes in. He reads and is wonderful. Everyone wants him, but ABC turns him down. A year later they're paying him a fortune to star in the miniseries *Rich Man, Poor Man*.

We cast Ricardo Montalban as the heavy. His part was mostly as an off-camera voice. He wasn't revealed until the last scene. I would dare say that there are maybe five voices in Hollywood that are instantly recognized. Ricardo's is one of the five.

We needed a female heavy to play opposite Cathy Lee. I pride myself on never having missed a day's work. But as luck would have it—bad luck, that is—I'm out the day the heavy is to be cast. I call in and tell Eddie Foy and John D. F. Black, "Look, it's great if she's good-looking, but she also has to look strong, and *she has to be athletic*. We'll have a stunt double for her, but Cathy Lee is very athletic, so the actress we hire has got to look believable in the fight scenes."

They both agree. I come in on Monday and ask if they've cast anyone as the heavy, Angela. They tell me that not only have they cast her, but that I'll be very happy with her because she's really an athlete. "She'll be in at two o'clock to meet you."

The production manager, Clarence Urist, comes in.

"Clarence, what do you think of the actress who's been cast for the role of Angela?"

"*The Price is Right.*"

"I don't care what they're paying her, what do you think of her?"

"*The Price is Right*! She's one of the models who shows the prizes on *The Price is Right*. Her name is Anitra Ford."

"Great."

Anitra comes in at two o'clock. She's about five eight and weighs, at the most, a hundred and twenty pounds. She's very attractive, but not athletic-looking. Anitra puts me at ease.

"Don't worry, John, I'm really working on the athletic parts. My boyfriend, Jim Brown, the football star, is helping me work out. We've been practicing in my garage."

"Sounds good, Anitra. What have you been practicing?

"Throwing the javelin."

"Throwing the javelin in your garage?"

That was an omen of things to come.

Barry Diller, who has gone on to become one of the biggest people in Hollywood, was the ABC contact person on the show. He and I didn't get along. It happened that he was right, and I was wrong. What else is new?

"John, the most important things in the show are the bracelets. I hope you are concentrating on this."

"Barry, I'm more interested in the stunts."

"No, it's the bracelets, the bracelets, the bracelets. They deflect bullets and perform magic."

"Okay, Barry."

I show him twenty pairs of bracelets. He finally picks one out. Then comes the belt, the boots, and so on.

We're finally going to start interviewing directors. We had sent the script to five directors, and we intended to set up a meeting with each of them. They all read the script; however, none of them wanted a meeting.

I realize that this is an opportunity to work with my good friend, Vince McEveety. I know he's going to be free around the time we'll need him. I mention him to John D. F. John goes to ABC, and everyone approves of Vince. I call Vince, who's shooting *Gunsmoke* at the time, and tell him about the great show I'm doing *(lie #1)*. He asks me to send him the script. I tell him I can't because it isn't quite finished *(lie #2)*. "Let me call Ronnie Leaf [his agent] and make the deal."

He agrees. I call Ronnie, who wants to see the script. "We don't have it completed" *(lie #3)*. I offer Ronnie a lot of money, and he accepts the deal.

Vince McEveety is still speaking to me, and we remain good friends to this day.

IF THE SCRIPT IS BAD, FILMING IT DOESN'T MAKE IT BETTER

The first day of shooting is on location at the Alexandria Hotel in downtown Los Angeles. We decorate the lobby to look like Cap d'Antibes. It looks very authentic. The first shot is of Cathy walking through the hotel lobby and up to the desk where she registers. The shot goes fine, as does the rest of the day.

The next day we're in the hotel again. I get a phone call from the studio. "John, you have, in your words, an 'opportunity.' In watching the dailies, nobody recognized Wonder Woman."

"Nobody is supposed to recognize her. She doesn't have the outfit on."

"No, John, she has to be recognized for being a presence."

"Oh, well."

I pass this information on to Vince. He has a fit. We shoot the scene several different ways. Extras looking at Cathy, comments being made about her, waiters turning around and staring at her.

The first shot of Cathy in her Wonder Woman costume is when she's on a landing on the Columbia Ranch backlot. She jumps to the ground and looks around. We're all wondering why she's looking around on a deserted street, and why she doesn't just get on with her business. Oh no, this is the way it must be.

The funniest incidents on *Wonder Woman* were in the "ooze room." We had a scene where we needed two walls to come together. Wonder Woman was trapped by the villain. As these walls came together, ooze would pour out of them. This was going to be an act-ender. The audience would think Wonder Woman had been crushed between the walls. In the next act, of course, they'd see how she miraculously escaped. It took three weeks to prepare the ooze room. Finally the day comes to film the scene. George, the special effects man, is ready. Vince recommends we run a test first while we're shooting another scene.

We hear a lot of noise and go over to where the test is being conducted. We see the walls slowly coming together. All of a sudden they collide and break! Not only do they break, but the ooze isn't coming out.

"George, how are we going to fix this?"

"Give me three days, and I'll be ready."

Three days later he says he's ready. We put Cathy between the two walls; the button is pushed; inch by inch the walls begin to come together to crush Wonder Woman. The ooze starts slowly coming out—but it comes out all over Cathy, ruining her hair and her costume. Luckily, she gets out. Meanwhile, the walls come together and break again.

"George, what happened?"

"I wish I could tell you."

At the end of the show, Ricardo is being taken off to jail. He has to say, "Wonder Woman, I love you." John D. F. orders Ricardo to say the line ten different ways. Ricardo is a great sport. "This is worse than my first screen test."

Every Saturday morning around nine o'clock, Vince McEveety would be the first to call. "John, I can't take it anymore, I'm quitting. Don't pay me, I quit!" After thirty minutes I would convince him to stay.

The next call would be from Cathy, crying. "John, I'm trying to be good. I'm doing the best I can, but I can't take this. Replace me. Do whatever you want, I'll give all my money back. I . . . I . . . I can't come in Monday, I can't take this anymore!" I'd finally convince her to come in Monday.

Last would be John D. F.'s call. "Everything is going beautifully. Now I want you to listen very carefully."

"To what?"

"Just listen."

On would come twenty minutes of symphonic music over the phone. Fortunately it was football season, and I'd be watching the game while I waited for the music to stop.

"Well, how'd you like that? That's the score for *Wonder Woman*."

"Sounds wonderful, John."

When a show is completed, the studio takes a rough cut and shows it to a studio audience. The audience members press buttons when they're excited and press other buttons for pathos, humor, and the like. When the screening is over, ten people are arbitrarily picked from the audience. They are taken to another room where an interviewer asks them what they did or didn't like about the show. In those days, this room would have two-way mirrors and the show's producers and executives would be seated in a sealed-off room above it where they, and only they, could watch and listen to the people below. The people commenting on the show wouldn't know they were being watched.

During the screening of *Wonder Woman*, there's a lot of laughter when there shouldn't be and very little pushing of buttons registering excitement. In the glass booth, the first question is, "Does anyone have anything to say about the show?" One fellow raises his hand.

"There's something I don't understand. I used to watch *Superman*. He'd go into a telephone booth as Clark Kent and come out as Superman. When Wonder Woman goes into a telephone booth, the bad guys run over it. Why does that happen?" Good question.

Next the interviewer asks, "Can we see a show of hands of how many of you would watch this show?"

Only one elderly lady raises her hand. "Yes, I'd watch it, but only if there wasn't anything else on that I wanted to watch."

"Give me an example of what show you would watch instead of *Wonder Woman*."

"A good hockey game."

When I was at CBS, our casting director on *Gunsmoke* was Pam Polifroni. During the hiatus time, she would get copies of film and TV shows to run, looking for talent. The people at *Gunsmoke* had heard about *Wonder Woman*, but no one had ever seen it. Everybody wanted to see if it was as bad as they had heard. Pam called Warner Bros. and asked to be sent a copy. She came back into our office. "This has never happened to me in all my years of casting. I called the film library at Warners and asked if I could get a copy of the pilot of *Wonder Woman*. The woman asked, 'Why would anybody want to watch that?'"

PREMIER SADAT—*GUNSMOKE*'S LAST SEASON

 *A*fter *Wonder Woman* I took a rest. During that time, I had a number of interesting offers. Probably the most interesting one was from a fellow from my church, Ed Griffin, who worked for Technicolor. He calls one day to tell me that Technicolor is putting together a show about Egyptology that will be filmed in Egypt. He had mentioned my name to the Technicolor people, and they want me to come talk to them.

I meet with the Technicolor people and they explain that the show will be filmed in Egypt and the postproduction will be done in London. They want me to take two or three people over to Egypt—my cameraman, Mike Joyce, and a couple of others. It sounds great. I ask if there is anything else for me to do.

"Yes, there is just one thing, and I know you'll enjoy it. It's filming openings and closings with Premier Sadat."

Now, I'm not that up on the situation in the Middle East, but I certainly know who Anwar Sadat is. "Is he going to say anything political?"

"No. Nothing political."

"Okay, Ed, I'll go home and discuss it with my family and call you tomorrow."

The next morning in the *Los Angeles Times*, the headline reads "Sadat Says All Jews Must Die!" I call Ed, who seems rather surprised when I turn the job down.

"Ed, I'll never work in Hollywood again if I have anything to do with Sadat."

Ed keeps after me, to no avail. How was I to know that there was going to be a Camp David, Anwar Sadat and Israel would make peace, and the film would run in conjunction with the Egyptology Tour, an exhibit which went all over the world?

I had a number of interviews with a number of people. None of them went that well. I remember Tom Laughlin was interested in having me work on *Billy Jack Goes to Washington*. His production manager calls me one night at 12:45 a.m.

"John, we've just come back from location. Tom wants you here in thirty minutes."

That was the end of my interest in working for the Laughlin group.

Finally I get a call from Eddie Denault, the head of production at CBS. "There's an opening on *Gunsmoke*, and I think you'd be perfect for the job."

"Me? Me on *Gunsmoke*? I don't think I've ever even seen *Gunsmoke*."

"Just go in there and meet with John Mantley."

"John Mantley? I sort of know him. Don Fedderson was going to do a Western with him." We had had a meeting, and Mantley was going on about how it had to be this, it had to be that, he wanted this, and he wanted that. Fedderson was sitting there kind of listening and nodding his head. The show never came to pass. "What do you want me to say to John Mantley?"

Eddie Denault comes out with some words of wisdom that I've found to be so true. "John, if you're going to have an interview with an extremely talented and powerful man, you don't have to say anything. He'll do most of the talking. All you do is sit and listen. Maybe answer a few questions. You'll be shocked at the result."

I meet with John Mantley, and basically John talks about John—everything from his Royal Canadian Air Force days to the present. I would guess that out of a thirty-minute interview, John speaks for twenty-eight minutes, and I speak for two. So much for that interview.

Ed Denault was right. The next day I get a call from CBS Business Affairs saying John Mantley wants to hire me. At this point, *Gunsmoke* had been on television for nineteen years. It first aired in 1955. I ended up working on the last thirteen episodes of what turned out to be the show's final season.

On *Gunsmoke,* I met types of people that I had never met before. Real cowboys! Not the Gene Autry and Roy Rogers type of cowboys I was raised on, but *the real thing!* James Arness, the star of the show, was six feet seven inches tall. His stunt double, Ben Bates, was six feet eight inches. Ben had been a Marlboro Man. The head wrangler, Dick Lundin, was the mustached man driving the six-up on the Wells Fargo commercials.

Although I'd worked with stunt people before, there is a big difference between cowboy stunt people and other stunt people. This was a new world to me, and I was a bit apprehensive. Friends encouraged me by saying, "Just do your job. Be organized, and everything will work out fine. The fights will be staged by the stunt people and the director; they all know what to do." I followed their advice.

On *Gunsmoke* we brought in a new, young director to do an episode. He comes down, meets everybody, and gets ready to do the first rehearsal with Jim Arness. It's a three-and-a-half page scene with Ken Curtis, who plays Festus. The rehearsal goes fine, and then the director says, "Okay, let's go for a take."

They do the take. When it's over, the director says, "Cut. Okay, that's good. I'd like to do one more. I think we can do a little better, Jim."

"Better? What do you mean, better? That's the best I can do. If you want better, get Larry Oliver" (Jim's rendition of Laurence Olivier).

The director is taken aback. He turns to me.

"Just say 'Cut, print.'"

"Cut. Print."

James Arness knew his character, Matt Dillon, better than anyone. He'd been playing Matt for twenty years. I think Jim downplayed how good an actor he really was. If Jim said "That's it," that was it!

After twenty years, the show was cancelled because we couldn't "make the point system." In the days of the point system, violence was the enemy. Every five or ten years both violence and sex go out. In TV, sex always comes back first. Violence follows. A point was deducted for every act of violence committed. For example, if Matt Dillon went into a bar and someone picked a fight with him, and he hit the guy and knocked him out, that was one point. If Matt and Festus were ambushed by twenty-five outlaws in a cabin, and wound up shooting and killing all twenty-five of them, that was one point. It never made any sense to any of us, but we had three points per episode and that was it. We tried to get below the three but couldn't. *Gunsmoke* was cancelled on April 25, 1974—the same day as John Mantley's birthday.

I HELP TO PUT *60 MINUTES* INTO PRIME TIME

Luckily for me, the day after *Gunsmoke* was cancelled, I had an offer to do a show for the Mary Tyler Moore company called *Three for the Road*.

It was the first single-camera show that the company was going to do. It was about a father and his two sons traveling all over the country in a motor home called "Z-Beck." Actually, due to ratings and budget restraints, the farthest they ever traveled was Monterey, California.

The cast of *Three for the Road* consisted of Alex Rocco, who went on to do a number of films and TV guest appearances; Leif Garrett, a singer-actor and former teen idol; and Vince Van Patten, who left the business to become a tennis player. The show, which only aired for the 1975 season, was doomed from day one.

The writer-producer was Jerry McNeely, a very talented writer who had come over from Universal Studios. The pilot was his idea, and CBS bought it. Sunday night was considered family night. Prime time began at 7:00 p.m. A lot of stations had the option to either pick up a show or not. Most of the stations chose not to pick up *Three for the Road*.

Unfortunately, Jerry McNeely's wife was ill, so he was seldom at the studio. He was constantly going back to Green Bay, Wisconsin, where he lived. He left us with a story editor, Nina Laemmle, a very nice lady, but one of the two story editors in all of Hollywood who didn't write. So there we were with a writer-producer who wasn't there and a story editor who didn't write. You can imagine how the scripts turned out.

The Mary Tyler Moore Company was famous for *The Mary Tyler Moore Show* and all of the other hit comedy shows produced there—*Bob Newhart* and *Rhoda*, to name just two. Its production manager, Abby Singer, was and is a true Hollywood legend. When I introduced people to Abby, they were surprised; no one believed there really was an Abby Singer. Abby actually has a film shot named after him. If someone says, "This is the Abby Singer shot," it means it's the next-to-the-last shot in a particular day's filming. The name came about when Abby went up to a director one time and asked him how many shots the director had left, and the director said, "This and one more." And Abby said, "How many shots do you have?" Obviously two.

Abby is the most penurious man I have ever met in my life—with the company's money. With his own money, he's very generous, but with the company's money, unbelievable! From the first location I go on, I call my assistant, Sally Hope, and ask her to get me a *Players Directory*. We're casting, and I have to approve some actors I'm not familiar with, and so I want to look them up in the book. Sally says, "Well, I'll have to ask Abby first. You know the *Academy Players* directories cost $35 apiece. We have two in the office, and I don't think he'll approve a third one."

She puts Abby on the phone. "John, we can't afford three *Players* directories at $35 apiece. You already have seven pens and, I believe, eight pencils, and now you're asking for $35 to get another *Players Directory*? It's absolutely ridiculous."

"Okay Abby, I'll just fly back and look at the books in the office when I don't know someone. That's a round-trip ticket to and from the location, but whatever you say."

I got the *Players Directory*.

My agent made the deal for me to do *Three for the Road*. I was to get so much in salary and so much in expenses. This was in my normal contract. All of a sudden I get on location, and there's no expense check. I call Abby. "John, they've changed their minds."

"How can they change their minds? It's in my contract."

"Don't worry about that, just charge whatever you want, and we'll reimburse you. But don't spend too much money."

Needless to say, this gets me a little upset. The first out-of-town location is in Monterey. I take the crew to the Sardine Factory, probably the most expensive restaurant in that area. I send Abby the bill, which is over $700. The next week I get my expense check as agreed upon in my contract.

The first production meeting with Abby was hysterical. The episode involved a tennis match. Tim Matheson was to be our guest star. It would be three matches with Vince Van Patten and Tim Matheson meeting in the finals. There would be the quarterfinals, the semifinals, and the finals. Abby had one phrase he always used when it came to how many people or how much you wanted for something: "Can't you go with . . ."

If you mentioned a hundred, he'd say can't you go with fifty. If you said you needed twenty cars, he'd say can't you go with ten. We start with the quarterfinal match.

"Abby, for the quarterfinal match, I think we should have seventy-five extras in the gallery."

"Can't ya go with fifty?"

I go with fifty.

"Abby, at the semifinals I think we should have one hundred and twenty-five there at least."

"Oh, that's too many, couldn't you go with seventy-five?"

"Maybe eighty-five, is that all right, Abby?"

"Can't ya go with eighty?"

"Okay."

Now, dumb as I am, I'm finally getting wise.

"Abby, for the finals, I need three hundred extras."

"No, Johnny, please. Can't you go with two hundred and twenty-five? That's the most I can give you."

"Abby, you'll ruin the show. Okay, we'll settle for two hundred and twenty-five."

That was the first and last time I ever got the best of Abby. I really only wanted two hundred.

I genuinely liked Abby, in spite of our disagreements. We are still friends today. He worked on and on for many years and did many shows. He has a very interesting theory about production, which a lot of people have. It's diametrically opposed to mine. His theory is to give everybody as little as possible in the way of equipment, and they'll make do with what you give them. My theory is have more than you need because if anything goes wrong, you're always prepared with a backup. Both theories exist to this day. Neither of these theories was invented by one of us. I've always thought that if Abby had gone up the mountain with Moses, they'd have come down with eight commandments!

At the end of the thirteen episodes of *Three for the Road*, CBS came to us. "You've done a good job. The public really loves you. [This was interesting because no one ever saw us.] But we're going to have to replace you."

Our show was replaced by a daytime show that they figured might do well in prime time. That show was *60 Minutes*. If our show hadn't been such a disaster, who knows where *60 Minutes* would be today?

JIM ARNESS AND *HOW THE WEST WAS WON*

My next adventure was working with John Mantley and James Arness again, on the miniseries *How the West Was Won*. My main job on the show, according to Jim Arness, was to find Jim a home, hire him a cook, and make sure there was a driver available to take him back and forth to the set when we were on location. The reason for all this was understandable. If Jim Arness walked down the streets of Manhattan, Los Angeles, or Chicago, he wouldn't get a second look. However, the locations where we had to film were where you'd find Jim's biggest fans. The people would crowd around him; he could never go out to dinner. His fans would be after him for autographs.

Jim had a few quirks. We could never be on a distant location when he had a day off. On Saturdays, which was the day he would leave to go home, he'd work until 11:00 a.m. and then be released and take off. On Saturday mornings the director would be surprised to find Jim on the set, in wardrobe, made up, and ready to go. Somehow we always moved quickly on those days. Jim had a plane pick him up every Saturday to fly him home. Being ornery, he wouldn't go directly home. Instead he'd have the plane circle our location, over and over. He knew we couldn't use any of the sound, so he'd wave at us, and we'd make gestures back at him. This happened every Saturday. We finally got the point. By rearranging the schedule, we were able to free Jim on Friday's last shot.

How the West Was Won was a classic Western. It told the story of the McMahon family—Zeb McMahon, his sister, and his deceased sister's three children. (No, this was not a Don Fedderson show!) Jim Arness played Zeb, a cavalry scout and Indian fighter.

I didn't do the pilot, but I did the rest of the shows, which aired from 1976 through 1978. The first year we did a six-hour miniseries. The supporting cast was Eva Marie Saint, Bruce Boxleitner, Will Hutchins, Kitty Holcomb, and Victoria Schreck. Harris Katleman was the head of MGM TV. The first shock we got was when we hired Burt Kennedy, the famous Western director, to direct. Eva Marie Saint was not overjoyed.

"No. I don't want to work with Burt Kennedy. I want a woman's director; I want Danny Mann. I've already told Harris."

John Mantley and I go to Harris Katleman's office. We've already hired Burt. This is two weeks before we're going to start filming, and we've already built the McMahon family home on locations in Kanab, Utah. We'll be there for eighteen days and then return to MGM to film for twenty days. Harris comes up with a shocker.

"By the way, I don't think you two have read Eva's contract."

"No, we were never sent a copy."

"Eva doesn't go on distant locations."

"What? Eva doesn't go on location? Harris, did you read the script?"

"Eva doesn't go on location." This means we have to shoot with Burt Kennedy in Kanab and duplicate the sets back in Los Angeles at the Hunter Ranch. "And as for the director, she gets Danny Mann."

"Harris, has Danny Mann ever shot a Western?"

"That doesn't make any difference, he's a director. He can certainly do Westerns."

Danny Mann comes in to meet John Mantley. "Danny, have you ever done Westerns?"

"Of course I've done Westerns. I can't remember the names of them, but I've done them." (He had actually done one.)

We go to the Kanab, Utah locations and shoot with Burt Kennedy. Everything goes smoothly. I learned a lot from Burt. He wants to shoot what looks like a tough day on the first day of filming. It was a spectacular-looking day that, with planning, we can actually get rather easily.

"This should please the network and the studio. They'll be off our backs for the remainder of the show. Give them something brilliant."

We start in with the massacre of the Indian village. It comes off great. We get the whole day's work done and send the dailies back to the studio. They love them. The network loves them. Everything is pretty much taken care of except that the production manager, Kurt Neumann, who had done a lot of big features, had forgotten to tell us that Harris Katleman wants to be called at home every day after the first shot. The next day we get the first shot at seven o'clock in the morning Utah time. This is six o'clock L.A. time. I call Harris at home to give him the news. That was the last time I had to call Harris.

Michael Daves is our first assistant director. We're lining up our biggest shot of the fourth day. We have to get the master shot before lunch. We have about thirty-five minutes to get it. It's a shot where the entire cavalry has to come into the fort in Kanab, and all of the actors have to get into position for the ensuing dialogue, while at the same time the Indians are exiting the fort. If we get the shot before lunch, we'll break for lunch for thirty minutes, then come back and not have to relight the entire set. We'll go right into coverage.

Everything is fine. I have to go make a phone call. Before I leave the set, Burt comes over to me. "No problem, John, we'll get it."

Then Jack Wolf, the cameraman, walks up. "No problem, we're going to get it."

I return from making my phone call in fifteen minutes. As I get back, I see the crew walking away. I say to the AD, "Michael, you got it, great. Good work."

"John, you're not going to be happy. We broke for lunch without getting the shot."

"You've got to be kidding!"

"No."

"What happened?"

"Jim wanted to go to lunch."

"What do you mean Jim wanted to go to lunch?"

"John, you know Jim's position in the scene. He's leaning against the gate as the cavalry is coming in. Just before the camera started rolling, Jim yelled out, 'Michael, I'm hungry!' John, I've got to please the star, so I called, 'Lunch, thirty minutes!'"

"Oh no!"

I go to Jim. "What did you do? You're not the assistant director. You don't call lunch."

"John, I didn't do anything. All I said was, 'I'm hungry,' which I am. I didn't call lunch, but when the AD calls lunch, I eat!"

We come back from Kanab a day ahead of schedule. We then encounter Eva Marie Saint and Danny Mann. All of a sudden, problems start to develop in the front office. John Mantley and Eva's husband, Jeff, take an immediate dislike to each another. There is a constant battle, which almost comes to fisticuffs. Jeff and I are producing the show, and he would come to me with various suggestions.

"John, the way those sets are painted is not going to work for Eva. The paint is not flattering to her; you'll have to change the colors."

I figure I have to make a stand right away. "Jeff, I'm not going to change the paint. It wouldn't make any difference. Check with the cameraman."

"That's your cameraman, but he doesn't know anything. I'm telling you it's wrong." I agree to change the paint.

Then Eva insists upon having her own writer for all of her dialogue. We get Jim Byrnes in to write all of Eva's material. In movies and TV, you have a script that originally starts out on white paper and then, as revisions are made, the new pages are run off on different colors—blue, pink, then yellow. This distinguishes the revisions from the original script. Jim Byrnes is rewriting all of the dialogue that's already been written and that the rest of the cast is going by. Everything has to come out of the MGM office where we are located and where John Mantley is. John takes all of Jim Byrnes' rewrites, and rewrites the rewrites. Then Eva gets the revisions.

"This seems to be the way it was before Jim Byrnes ever rewrote it."

Eva obviously also has copies of Jim Byrnes's rewrites. She compares them and calls me over. "John, I'm not going to shoot until I get Jim Byrnes out here."

Jim Byrnes comes out, but John Mantley can't because Eva has barred him from the set. "If he comes on the set, I'll leave."

The Saturday morning phone calls start with Eva. It's seven o'clock.

"John, Eva. John, why don't we ever have brownies for dessert?"

"Well, Eva, I really never thought about it."

"Well, I want brownies for dessert."

"Fine, Eva, we'll have brownies every day."

"I didn't say every day! I'll let you know Monday night what dessert I want for Tuesday."

One day we're shooting at nearby Hunter Ranch. In the middle of a shot, Jeff comes driving up and slams on the brakes, wrecking the shot.

"Eva, Eva, they're ruining you. They're making you look terrible." Eva goes into a tantrum and runs out.

In addition to keeping the show going, another part of my job was to be friendly with Jeff, which really wasn't that difficult. I'm sure he meant well in his own way. It's just that people have different means of getting their ends accomplished, so to speak. We finally calm Eva down. Jeff has a discussion with the cameraman and of course, they hear about it at MGM. Just as we're finally getting ready to start filming again, a helicopter appears and hovers overhead, making it impossible to film. Then the helicopter lands. Out steps Harris Katleman. He walks over to me to find out what's going on. I tell him everything has been settled, and we're attempting to finish the day's work.

"Hi Eva, I've settled everything. If you need anything else, call me at the studio."

He gets back in the helicopter and flies away. Another two-and-a-half hours lost.

We were scheduled to shoot in Kanab for eighteen days and to film at the Hunter Ranch for twenty days. We got back from Kanab in seventeen days and finished the Hunter Ranch part in thirty-five days.

One day, Danny asks me to go over the rest of the week's filming. "Now it says this, and it says that in the script . . . "

"Danny, what script are you reading?"

"This one."

I look at his script. It's all white pages: it's the original script. He has no idea what the blue, yellow, or pink pages are so when he gets them, he just throws them out. It takes quite a lot of explaining because here is a man who has directed on Broadway and has directed shows at MGM that were mostly adaptations of stage plays. He would take four weeks of rehearsal and when he would go into production, all of the script pages would be white.

Danny didn't understand about working with children either, especially children doing their offstage dialogue. "Danny, if we have the children do their own offstage dialogue, we'll run out of time with them. That's why we have a dialogue coach. She'll read the children's lines when the children are in school or at recreation. Danny, if we do it your way, we'll be here for eighty days."

So Danny knew Westerns?

"John, I've got this great shot for tomorrow. Does it make a difference from which side someone mounts a horse?"

Things went on like that. When the six-hour miniseries was finished, everybody was scared to death. No one really knew what we had the last day of the show. John Mantley and James Arness had already agreed that Eva wasn't going to be back for the second season. We had to do a famous last scene where Jim was on horseback separated from Eva. We did this so that we could reshoot the end of the scene in such a way that it would end with Eva going off without Jim. Then we'd have a voice-over that would cover Eva not being in the rest of the series. This would allow us to bring in someone else for the next group of shows. Of course, no one told Eva about this. We had to slip it by her.

Jim had been great during all of these problems and putting up with Eva. That is, until the last day. All of a sudden, Jim and Eva get into an argument over some petty thing about coming in and out of a door and which way they should come in and go out. I guess Jim had really had it. I take him aside and try to calm him down. "Jim, if she walks off, it'll be hours before we find her. Besides, I'm out of brownies." He goes back, and we finish the scene.

Eva questioned the positioning in the final scene. We finally convinced her that there would be stunt doubles, and it would all work out fine. She bought it, and the rest of the series was sans Saint.

Both John Mantley and Jim Arness were out of town when the show aired. Fred Silverman, the man in charge of ABC at the time, calls the next morning. I'm the only one in the office.

"Congratulations! You're number one in the Nielsens!"

SEASON TWO OF *WEST*

*E*veryone returned from their vacations to bask in the glory. It's possible that the reason we were number one was not only because *How the West Was Won* was a good show, but also because the show that had aired the week before was the final installment of a miniseries called *Roots*. During the *Roots* finale there were numerous promos for our show. These promos were seen by millions of people.

The next season was a twenty-hour continuing story that was really a doozy. We only had two directors, Vince McEveety and his brother Bernie. We had a lot of interesting people guesting on the second season. Ricardo Montalban was one. He was still talking to me and laughing about the *Wonder Woman* experience. We brought in Fionnula Flanagan, who took the part that Eva Marie Saint had had. The rest of the cast was the same.

I met some real cowboys on their ranches. They're interesting people. They have their own code of justice, which I'm sure dates back to the old West. They'd never sign a contract. If I wanted to film on a ranch, and the rancher was there, I'd make the deal with him. There'd be a handshake and that was that.

Some of the cowboys' habits were unbelievable. When I'd go to scout the ranches, I'd usually meet the guys at five o'clock in the morning. They'd always be sitting at breakfast with a pack of either Camels or Marlboros, smoking away and drinking their coffee, which was heavily laced with bourbon.

"Here, ya gotta have some of this coffee."

Well, what was I going to do? I'd drink the coffee.

We had some interesting casting situations on locations. We'd cast some people. I'd come back three days before we were going to shoot, and I'd see guys with black eyes and broken arms. "What happened? You're going to work in three days!"

"Well, I got in a fight. It was Saturday night. That's what we do here on Saturday nights. I broke my arm, and my friend got a black eye."

We just had to remember that those were the things that go on in those places.

One time we needed to cast a fellow to wrestle with Jim Arness. He has to be a big, burly Russian. Sally Hope and I are casting up in Denver, Colorado. We're sitting down in the orchestra pit. The runway is up above us with all of these people parading by. All of a sudden this big, powerful-looking guy comes along who's exactly what we're looking for. He says he's done professional wrestling. Perfect! He gives us his picture. We cast him and take his picture back to MGM. They're really excited. "Where did you find this guy? This is going to be sensational!"

Two days before filming is scheduled to start, we're back in Colorado. We're in the town of La Junta, which is where we're going to shoot. The director, Bernie McEveety, and I are walking across the street to have dinner.

"John, that little man in front of us, isn't he the Russian wrestler you cast?"

I walk up to the guy to get a good look, and sure enough it's him. I've made a big mistake! The fellow is about five feet five inches tall and he weighs about 280 pounds. He's really built, but when we cast him, we were looking up at him from the orchestra pit as he walked by on the runway. We had no idea he was that short. I have to tell him that I've made a mistake, explaining that we can't have someone five feet five wrestle someone who's six feet seven. We pay him and have to start the search all over again.

This isn't easy in La Junta, Colorado. Here I am, in the middle of nowhere at five o'clock in the morning. I'd heard there was a "mountain man's" retreat and I'm walking around when I see this huge man in front of me. He's about six feet six or six feet seven and really muscular. I'm thinking, I don't care what his face looks like. This is the guy. I've got to get him. I walk up to the man and tell him who I am and what I want.

"Oh yeah, ah hah, sure, of course, yah, would you git on, I got things to do."

"Wait, here's a hundred-dollar bill. Take this money, write down the address of this office and go there. Tell the person at the desk that John Stephens cast you. They'll give you a contract to sign, and everything will be done."

As he walks away (upwind), I'm thinking, boy, this guy really is a mountain man, I don't think he's bathed for a month. I'm sure the office emptied when he got there. He did the part and was great.

One of the things about *How the West Was Won* was that we had to work in cities that were extremely remote. We couldn't shoot in many directions in any major cities due to the cable lines, telephone poles, highways, etc. We had to go to some of the smaller cities in America that you may never have heard of: Kanab, Utah; Chama, New Mexico; and La Junta, Colorado, to mention a few.

Chama, New Mexico is a city that everybody should go to once. We had to shoot nine days on a train there. It was all second unit, meaning that no cast principals were involved. We needed a three-gauge railroad, and Chama was the only place that had one.

We go there and start filming. We head back to our motel at the end of the first day, all filthy. There are only two motels in the town. I go to my room and get ready to take a shower. I look for the shower, and there isn't one, only a small bathtub. I go back out to the desk and ask about the shower. I'm told the other motel has showers, but this one doesn't.

"Look at me, I'm dirty from head to toe; how am I suppose to clean up?"

"You saw that bucket next to the tub? Just fill it up with hot water and dump it all over your head. You'll be all cleaned up."

I'm ready for dinner and find out there's only one restaurant in town, a steak house. You learn if you're doing cowboy shows, going to those towns, you'd better like steak because that's all you are going to get. We had nine days of that. No, I didn't become a vegetarian.

Another thing about doing Westerns is location scouting. This is probably the toughest part of the job and is done before the crew arrives. Somebody says we're looking for a fort, and the local location person says, "Oh, we've got a great fort for you." You get in the car, and you're driving with three cowboys and one of the local people. The cowboys start an argument about how much they sold a horse for, eight years ago.

"You sold that horse for $10."

"I sold it for $6."

"I'm telling you, you sold it for $10."

This is the type of dialogue you're listening to for about ninety miles. You finally arrive at the fort. It's totally barren ground with a few rocks scattered around. "What's this?"

"This was a fort."

"It was a fort, but it's not now. There isn't anything here but a few rocks."

"Well, couldn't you rebuild it?"

You get back in the car and go back the ninety miles you came from and go sixty more miles in the other direction. Maybe there'll be a fort. The reason we filmed so much in Kanab, Utah was they still had one of the only working forts.

The nights in these towns were murder. Take Kanab for instance. I am not a gourmet eater, and I'm not a drinker but all the same, if someone were to put you on a camel in the middle of a desert and say, "Look, there's only a little bit of water in that canteen, and you've got a hundred miles to go, so make sure you drink it sparingly," all of a sudden you'd have to have a drink of water. If you find you can't get a good meal, you want a good meal.

The people in Kanab were very unusual. There was our contact man, Fay Vincent. He was a "Jack Mormon." That meant he wasn't allowed in the inner temple. He drank, smoked, and did everything else he wasn't supposed to do. The local people didn't care that much for Fay. It was hard to get certain things from them. Fay passed away, and Merrill McDonald took over. Merrill was a true Mormon. He could get us anything we wanted.

The people in Kanab were dead set in their ways, very bigoted, to put it mildly. We had a guy named Willy, an African-American, as our sound boom man. In those days you could drive your car to location. Willy had a problem with his bumper. The only thing of renown in Kanab is one of the largest bumper shops in the world. Willy drives into the place to get a new bumper. They won't give him one. Willy calls me, and we go down to the place together. We see the exact bumper Willy needs.

"What's the problem?"

"No problem. We're not selling him a bumper. "

We go back to the office, and I call John Earl, the head of all Utah filming, and tell him what's going on. "John, you gotta just let that go."

"No, I don't have to just let that go. I'll tell you what, either Willy gets that bumper by tomorrow morning, or I'm going to take this whole company out of Kanab and the state of Utah." Willy got the bumper the next morning.

I understand Utah has changed a lot since then, but for me, you can have Kanab, Utah!

SEASON THREE—BURGESS MEREDITH NEEDS TOILET PAPER

I got to know John Mantley very well on this show. He was absolutely brilliant, but he had to have a hand in *everything*. For example, we would have people come in and read for parts. John always wanted to read opposite the actors and actresses. This was especially tough on the actors.

One day Tom Selleck comes in to read for a part. In the scene he's telling his girlfriend that he can't marry her. The script calls for the actress to break down and cry. John Mantley is reading the actress's part, and it's difficult for Tom to respond to John, who's not only crying and using a falsetto voice but is trying to out-act the actor. Tom leaves and John remarks, "I don't think he's right at all; he doesn't have any emotion."

"John, you're the executive producer. You already have a job. We need an actor for this part. Could you just tone down your emotion in the reading?" Tom Selleck went on to prove John wrong.

John had a way of projecting himself into everything. One time near the end of the season we filmed a buffalo stampede. We shot it in a beautiful location, with mountains in the background and flowing water. John was very proud of this scene. I got constant calls from John while I was on location, telling me you have to do this, you have to do that.

I'm back at MGM and John is showing the rough-cut footage we had filmed of the location to the studio heads. John pipes up, "You can't believe how I picked this location. It's magnificent, and I knew everybody would love it" and on and on.

Now, I'm tired and getting madder and madder at him. Finally something snaps. "John you never even saw this location until you came during filming!"

He got very angry, rightly so. I thought I had learned not to dress down anyone in front of others, but that all went out the window, and I embarrassed John in front of the execs. I should have known better.

Another time we need someone to paddle a canoe across a lake in the early dawn. With the wind, it's a very difficult shot. We get it about 4:45 a.m. I get a call from John Mantley the next day. He starts telling me, "We'll get letters from the American Canoe Association because the actor kept changing the position of the paddle, and you don't do that. Where did you ever find that guy? We're going to have to reshoot the whole scene."

"John, when we get the first letter from the American Canoe Association, if there is such an association, then fine, we'll reshoot it somewhere else, I promise." Of course, we never got a letter.

There are about five of us driving to lunch one day in Culver City. We had been looking for an Indian to play a part. John spots this Indian getting onto a bus in Culver City. "John, there he is! John, quick, get on that bus, find that Indian, we need him!"

I jump out of the car, barely make it onto the bus, and walk down the aisle looking for the "Indian." When I spot him, I introduce myself and give him my pitch. He looks at me in disbelief. "Are you serious?"

"I am."

He reaches into his briefcase and pulls out his eight-by-ten photo. "Here, contact my agent."

In season three, we're going to do an episode called "Billy Fargo" about an old prospector. It's mostly a two-person story with the characters Luke, played by Bruce Boxleitner, and Billy Fargo. We're looking for the best old-time star we can find to play the prospector. Burgess Meredith's name comes up. That sounds good, he's a great actor, let's get him. Of course, with Burgess Meredith, along came Barney McNulty and his cue cards. Barney McNulty was a fabulous fellow who revolutionized TV with his cue cards. I believe his card system was far better than any teleprompter. Poor Barney, every time we worked together, it was with a difficult person. And if you were to spell "difficult" it would be spelled B-u-r-g-e-s-s M-e-r-e-d-i-t-h!

We're on location in Canon City, filming. Burgess comes up to join the cast. He meets Vince McEveety, the director.

"You're the director. Here's what you're going to do. Tell me which hand to carry my gun in and how you want my hat cocked, but don't ever try to direct me. I direct myself when it comes to my acting. Do you have that straight?" That was the start of things to come.

After hearing this, I decide that instead of going back to the office, I'll hang around the set in the back, with a cowboy hat on, observing unobtrusively. I don't want to get involved in their problems. The first day goes okay. After every take where Vince says "Print!" Burgess says, "We're doing another one." It ends up with Burgess being the one to say "Print." Vince is really going crazy.

The second day, Burgess is complaining about something in his room, and Vince gets this bright idea. "You should talk to John Stephens about that."

"Who's that?"

"That's the producer."

"Producer? I never saw a producer here."

Vince points to me. "That guy there is the producer."

"Producer? I thought he was some wrangler or something."

Burgess walks over to me. "Listen, producer, I don't like the toilet paper in my room. It's too coarse. I want you to get that changed. And I don't like the food from room service; can you do anything about that?"

I tell him I'll take care of everything. Big mistake! Burgess calls me constantly, complaining about this, complaining about that. He doesn't like anything. I'm very thankful that he'll only be with us for seven days. On his last day, I'm excited at the prospect of his leaving, as is the entire cast and crew. Barney McNulty comes to me just before we're going to wrap, to tell me that Burgess is throwing a party that night for Vince and me in his motel room.

Burgess had always been talking about going on boats, going to wine-tasting events, how he's a gourmet chef, etc. We figure we'll get a decent meal in Canon City someplace besides Gus's, the only restaurant in town. We arrive at his room and there's some cheap Chablis, a few crackers, and a little bit of cheese. We keep waiting for food to be brought in by room service. None comes. That was Burgess's idea of a party.

MARCIANO AND WORKING WITH BOXERS

My next project was a movie of the week, *Marciano*. It was the story of Rocky Marciano, the undefeated heavyweight champion. The show was a combination of fact (Rocky's prizefights) and fiction (his life story). We shot it in 1979.

The script, written by Paul Savage, was one of the best scripts I had ever been given. Bernie Kowalski, a friend of mine for years, was hired to direct. I was hired to produce. Our casting director at ABC Circle Films was Pam Dixon. Pam had definite ideas.

"Kurt Russell will be perfect for this part."

"But Pam, he doesn't look like Marciano."

"So what? Who remembers what Marciano looked like?"

Kurt Russell had just come off playing Elvis Presley. Bernie and I agreed to go with him. Kurt Russell didn't. He didn't want to do another biographical role so soon after playing Elvis.

One of the actors we consider is Kevin Dobson, who did the *Kojak* series. His agent sends over a movie of the week that Kevin had recently done. It was about a man who had just had a massive heart attack and was home recovering. The woman playing Kevin's wife totally dominated the show. Bernie turns to me.

"Maybe we should use her to play Marciano. She's better than anyone else we've seen."

"Yeah, but don't you think she chews up the scenery? If she overacts, she'll never get anywhere."

That actress was Meryl Streep. Told you she'd never get anywhere.

We finally wound up casting Tony Lo Bianco. The only problem with Tony Lo Bianco was his age. We started the show with Rocky being nineteen years old. I don't know how old Tony was at the time, but he was probably closer to thirty-nine than nineteen.

I proceeded to make another error. We got in touch with Jimmy Jacobs, a fellow who owned a huge library of old prizefight films. Jimmy and I had lunch, and he agreed to let us view the films to get the feel of Marciano's fights. The mistake I made was letting Tony Lo Bianco see the films. I then went back to Brockton, Massachusetts, to meet with Rocky's brother, Peter. He had just gotten out of prison. He told me in no uncertain terms exactly how the show should be shot, what the story should be. He wanted final script approval. We didn't film in Brockton.

There were also tremendous problems regarding Rocky's late wife, Barbara. She had a drinking problem, and the Marciano family didn't want us to portray this in any way. In those days if there was an objection by the family, even though the facts were true and on record, no one at ABC wanted to risk a lawsuit. We had to change the story around and have Barbara Marciano have an undisclosed illness that continued all through the film. Rocky was constantly worried about his wife's health.

At the end of the film, Rocky gets on an airplane. The plane takes off, and then we cut to the phone ringing in Barbara's bedroom. We presume the audience will know that Rocky had died in a plane crash. Nobody got this. We had to go back and shoot another scene to end the show where Rocky and Barbara were running along the beach, supposedly in heaven. No one got this either.

During the filming, Tony, after viewing the Jimmy Jacobs's films, kept insisting on doing everything the way it happened. We'd have a camera set up, we'd be lit, and ready to go. Tony would then go back to his dressing room and view the Jacobs's film.

"Guys, you have to change the setup. Rocky didn't go down in this corner, he went down in that one." This happened time and time again.

Bernie insisted on using professional boxers instead of stuntmen. Professional boxers are strange people. When the bell rings, they know to go out and fight. When the bell rings again, they stop. When there's no bell, you don't know what they're going to do. We're filming in the Grand Olympic Auditorium in Los Angeles. The assistant director comes up to me.

"You know that fellow that's going to be fighting at noon today?"

"Yeah."

"Well, it's eleven-thirty, and he's leaving. You'd better go talk to him."

I hurry over to the guy. "Pardon me, where are you going?"

"What do you mean, where am I going? My wife is suing me. I gotta get to court!"

When the show finally aired, it went over like a lead balloon. Rocky Marciano was a great prizefighter but an extremely dull man. He trained

365 days a year, there were no women, no booze, and nothing but train-ing. His life didn't make for an interesting TV show.

The reason Marciano was killed in a plane crash was his extreme frugality. He had a round-trip ticket to fly on a major airline to give a speech in the Midwest. He cashed in the ticket and then talked a friend of his, a licensed pilot, into flying him in his single-engine plane. Imag-ine, a man worth millions of dollars trying to save a few bucks. The con-ditions he took off in were terrible. No major airline would have flown in that weather. The rest is history.

MEETING WITH BRANDON TARTIKOFF

*W*hile I'm at ABC Circle doing the postproduction on *Marciano*, I get a phone call from Paul Freeman, who at that time was working for a company called Landsburg Productions. Paul had been our NBC repre-sentative on *The Brian Keith Show* in Hawaii.

"John? What are you doing now? The company I work for knows all about you, and they really like you."

"What does that mean, Paul?"

"It means that we want you to come up with a show for us."

"Paul, I'm not a creator. I don't do that. I physically produce the shows. I'm not a writer."

"No, you can do it. Just send us over five pages or so on anything you can come up with."

"Paul, I'm not going to do that. I'll talk to you later, thanks for calling."

He starts phoning me every day. Finally I say to my assistant, "Look, Sally, on our lunch hour let's just get this done. We'll send him five pages and get this over with."

We write five pages of the worst drivel in the world: a mixture of shows I'd done at Fedderson plus a few of my personal shortcomings. There's the hero of the show; his ex-wife, a goody-two-shoes type who has divorced him because he's a drinker and a heavy gambler; and a daughter who is a Jane Fonda type.

Sally is in shock. "You're not really going to send this!"

"Yes, just to get rid of him, send it!"

We send it and three days later, Paul calls me. "John, we got the story. We want to buy it right away."

"Okay, Paul, what's the joke?"

"John, we love it. We want to buy it. Who's your agent?"

"Herb Tobias."

"I'll call him right now."

A half-hour later, Herb Tobias calls me. "Did you write something for Landsburg Productions?"

"Yeah, I did."

"They want to buy it from you."

"You're kidding."

"No. They want to pay you $10,000 for the story and then make a deal with you to produce the pilot. If the pilot goes, they want you to produce it. I never knew you wrote."

"Neither did I. Look, take the money, and let's go from there."

About five days later I hear from Paul Freeman telling me they want to meet me at Landsburg. I go over and meet with them. They're telling me what a great idea this is and how they'll love working with me. I'm sitting there, not knowing why I'm sitting there. All of a sudden they get around to why I'm there. "John, Brian Keith is a good friend of yours, isn't he?"

"More or less."

"Do you think Brian might be interested in this show?"

"I don't know."

"Would you call him?"

"Sure, I'll call him."

"John, if Brian's interested in this show, we can make a quick deal. Call him and let us know right away."

A big lightbulb goes off! "Okay."

I go home and call Brian in Hawaii. Cleaning up the expletives, Brian agrees to do the show. "If you want to do it, fine, sounds good to me. In other words I'm playing part of your life and part of my life. You're the gambler, and I'm the drinker. Why not? We'll make a lot more money. Work it out with my agent. We'll do it!"

I call Paul the next day.

"Great, just a minute . . . okay, can you come in here this Friday, and we'll set up a meeting . . . wait a minute, you don't have to come in, hold it. Let's set up a meeting with Brandon Tartikoff, who is the new program head of NBC. They love Brian there, and we'll pitch the idea to him."

Paul calls back five minutes later. "We have a meeting with Brandon on Monday."

"Fine." I still can't believe all this.

On Monday, we get to Brandon's office. He's very young, in his twenties, and has just been made the program head of NBC. He hasn't had that many meetings. I'm sitting outside his office with Meryl Grant, Alan Landsburg, and Paul Freeman. Instead of the usual tea, coffee, or soft drinks, Brandon's secretary offers us a box of See's Candy. This really impresses me. We're ushered into Brandon's office and meet Brandon and his assistant. Everything goes fine. He wants to hear the pitch, and we give it to him.

"This is sensational, this is really great. This is original. Listen, we have a deal. Why don't you think about any changes you want to make to this; we'll think of any changes we want to come up with, and let's set a meeting for next Tuesday at the same time. I'll call Business Affairs and tell them to be ready to close the deal. We'll definitely have a deal. This show is going to be on the air."

We walk out of Brandon's office. I'm stunned.

"Hey, we did it! Right, John?"

"I guess."

Cut to the chase. We go back to Brandon's office the following Tuesday. "Guys, we've got a deal. We're going to be on the air. We spoke to Business Affairs to work out all the financial arrangements. I know you guys are going to be happy with everything. We only have one change to your idea, John, and I'll let my assistant tell you about it because he came up with it."

Brandon's assistant—I've forgotten his name and assume this was his first and last suggestion—turns to me. "You know, John, there are a lot of shows where the wife leaves the husband because he was a ne'er-do-well, he gambles, he drinks, etc. I have a different take on this, and Brandon thinks it's a great idea."

"Yes, I do. Tell John about it."

"The reason Brian's wife left him is not because he's a drinker and a gambler, but . . . how's this, she left him because he's simply dull and boring."

I'm waiting for the laughs. Okay, what's the punch line, everybody's going to laugh. Nobody's laughing, this guy is serious. Suddenly, Landsburg jumps up.

"I think that's a great idea."

I'm still not believing my ears.

"Don't you think that's a great idea, John?"

"It's wonderful, absolutely wonderful, I can't wait to do this show."

We go out to the hallway.

"Congratulations, John. You must be very happy."

"I'll tell you what I'll do. You've given me $10,000. Give me a piece of paper, and I'll sign over all the rights to you. Not only that, I'll give you Brian Keith's home phone number in Hawaii. You call him and tell him that he's playing a character, week after week, who is so dull and boring that his wife left him. I'm sure he's going to love it."

The show was never made. Brandon went on to lead NBC back to being the number one network in the ratings and was considered a brilliant executive.

ELIZABETH MONTGOMERY AS DORIAN GRAY?— I ENTER THE 25TH CENTURY

I stayed at MGM to do a pilot film, *Buffalo Soldiers*. It was a pilot MGM had already made. It hadn't sold. They wanted me to redo it. Then they had a change of heart and cancelled the remake. Sally and I were there on a six-month contract with nothing to do. Then along came a once-in-a-lifetime project. At the time the man in charge of production at MGM was Peter Andrews. "John, I want you to sit and watch at least two old movies a day. See what you think would make a good movie of the week."

Sally called a good friend of hers and mine, Rudy Behlmer, a renowned author and film buff, for suggestions of movies we should watch. Our plate was full; we watched two, sometimes three movies a day. After four months, I have a meeting with Peter.

"Peter, I feel we can narrow it down to two that I think would make good Movies of the Week."

"Which ones, John?"

"Let's start with *The Picture of Dorian Gray*. When they first made it, there were so many restrictions you couldn't really do justice to Oscar Wilde's novel. Today you can."

"What a great idea, John. But instead of using a man, let's use Elizabeth Montgomery. She has a high TVQ, and that's what we want."

I start to tell him about my next idea when he interrupts me.

"John, you've done a number of Westerns, haven't you? [Ha!—here I am, known as a Western producer.] Remember the movie *Ride the High Country?*"

"Of course. It starred Joel McCrea and Randolph Scott. My neighbor, Dick Lyons, produced it. It's a classic."

"It sure is. Let's remake it, but instead of using two old guys, because that doesn't go today, let's make it two young guys."

"Good idea, Peter. Instead of two old guys on their last ride, we'll make it two young guys on their first ride."

I walked out of his office. Peter was out of his office two months later.

John Mantley had moved over to Universal to do *Buck Rogers in the 25th Century.* On October 11, 1980, Sally and I joined him on the show.

Universal was a rather interesting studio. John Mantley once said of the place, "At Universal they defy you to make a show. Any cooperation you expect, you can forget it. They argue about pennies and nickels and let the dollars go floating by."

I meet Gil Gerard, the star of *Buck Rogers.* The studio had said they were having a lot of trouble with him. "Don't give him anything." That was their standard line with all their television actors and actresses. Gil Gerard launches into his main complaint.

"Little Joe cuts my hair. He does haircuts for many of the stars, charging $35. The studio won't pay for it."

"Don't worry, Gil, I'll take care of it."

During the first week of shooting, Little Joe comes in to give Gil a haircut. He finishes, and I hand him $35. I get a call from Pete Terranova, a tower executive.

"You're new here, and you'd better not be pulling this stuff again, or you're never going to get old here."

I call the head of production, Bert Astor, to introduce myself. "I'm John Stephens, and I'll be working with John Mantley on *Buck Rogers.* I'd like to meet you."

"Why?"

"We'll be working together, and I like to meet the people I work with."

"Now we've met." He hangs up.

We later became good friends, and he was a tremendous help to me at the studio.

Buck Rogers was in its second season. The show was a TV version of the comic strip. In the one and only season I helped produce it, we recycled old *Gunsmoke* scripts, moving the characters from horseback to spaceships. I can't imagine why this didn't work!

I was introduced to David O'Connell, who was the producer on the show. A nice man, and, I'm sure, a capable producer. He knew post-production, but he knew nothing about production. Cal Clements, the story editor on *How the West Was Won*, came over as a producer. He didn't know how to produce, but he wanted the producer title.

I get in early one morning and check things out on the set. Somebody is putting the main "pit" in the wrong place for the bad guys to be in. I go to the construction foreman. "Who told you to put the pit here?"

"One of the producers. There's so many on this show that I can't remember which one."

I go to see David O'Connell. David leaves the show the next day.

Universal told me the first season was a disaster, and they were sure the second season would be too. I was informed that we had only six days to do each show. I was trained that if you have six days to make a show, you make the show in six days. It's that simple. We made *Gunsmoke* in six days, and certainly we were going to do *Buck Rogers* in six days. Besides, all of the postproduction in *Buck Rogers*, including all effects, would be put in later. We completed the first show, and it was reviewed. The review not only criticized the show, but also Gil Gerard and the lady star of the show, Erin Grey. Gil and Erin this, Gil and Erin that. Gil got furious.

"We're not Lunt and Fontanne. I'm the star of the show. Why do they keep putting me with her? If she can't act, that's her problem. I can act."

Wilfrid Hyde-White, who had appeared in *My Fair Lady* with Rex Harrison, among other big feature films, played the old professor in Buck Rogers. He was elderly then, and *Buck Rogers* was a number of years later, and Wilfred was a little more elderly. He introduces himself to me.

"I understand we're going out to Vasquez Rocks. Well, it's too hot for me out there, I can't go. I'm an elderly man, I can't go."

"You're in the scenes, you have to go."

"Well, make sure you have plenty of air conditioners for me because it's going to be so hot."

We made sure we had air conditioners; we did everything we could to make him comfortable. Wilfred was a constant complainer. He complained going onto the set, he complained on the set, and he complained walking off the set. He had no idea what he was doing; he'd just go through the lines and then about two o'clock, "I'm too tired and have to go home."

A month later, we had to reshoot the scenes out at Vasquez Rocks. Wilfrid started worrying about the cold. I told him not to worry, we had a heater in his room. The same thing happened. I guess the cold got to him more than the heat because at 11:30 a.m., he had to leave. We figured this might happen, and had him on the set earlier than necessary so we could get all of his coverage before he left. This went on day after day.

On top of everything else, the directors were going crazy because Wilfrid read every line exactly the same way. At one point, the director, Bernie McEveety, throws up his hands. "Wilfred, in this scene, you're probably seeing Buck for the last time as he's going to his death. You can't say 'Well dear boy, jolly well and all that.' This man is going to be killed."

"Well, good luck, dear boy, cheerio, and all that."

We cut this scene out of the show.

Wilfrid was always complaining about the work schedule and how tired he was. He's in my office one day around 5:00 p.m.

"John, can I use your phone to call my agent?" He dials a number. "Have you got me booked to do those voice-overs at Disney? You have. Well, let's see, it's five-fifteen now, yes, I can be there at seven. Two hours? Seven to nine? That's fine, I'll be there." No wonder he was always tired!

As the season progressed, the ratings got lower. Gil got more and more upset. Erin never got upset. Erin would come up to me on Friday and ask, "John, can I get out of here early today? I have a modeling job in Rome and if I can get out of here by noon, I can fly to Rome, do my modeling job and be back ready to go Monday morning. It means about $10,000 to me."

Gil on weekends was another story. I've never before or since encountered anyone with Gil's particular problem. He'd say good night to us on Friday, leaving the set weighing around 175 pounds. He'd come in Monday morning weighing 205 pounds. I have no idea what the chemical makeup of his body was. We had five of Gil's costumes in different sizes.

Another member of the cast, who went on to win daytime Emmys for soaps, was Thom Christopher. He played a character that John Mantley created called Hawk. He was absolutely the most ridiculous-looking personage on prime time TV when he put on the outfit that John had designed for him. He'd walk around with a tail, horns, and a long beak. Unbelievable.

"John, do you think this is going to ruin my career? Do you think I'll ever work again?"

"Thom, no one watches the show. Just don't put it on your résumé because someone may ask to see one of the episodes."

When *Buck Rogers* was finished, I was asked to do a show called *Simon & Simon* with Phil DeGuere. I didn't know anything about it. Earl Bellamy, who was actually my boss at Universal and the head of physical production for all of Universal television, told me he had set up the pilot for me to look at and to get back to him. I took Sally with me to see the pilot.

"How can they possibly make a pilot about two lawyers? What's funny or exciting about that?"

THE START OF *SIMON & SIMON*

We start watching, and I see Gerald McRaney, whom I had worked with many times. He acted in numerous *Gunsmoke* and *How the West Was Won* shows. Gerald was a one-day player. I always used to tease him.

"You know, you're making a big mistake because all the parts you play have you riding into town to kill the hero. You have a gunfight with him, and you're killed the first day. If you were the sheriff on the side of the law, you might get a three- or four-day run out of these shows."

The other lead actor is Jameson Parker. I've never heard of him. He was a soap opera star.

As Sally and I watch the pilot, we're pleasantly surprised. It's about two down-and-out brothers in San Diego working as private detectives.

The show is fast-paced, very hip, and very good. I've never done any-thing like it. It looks like it would be fun.

I meet with Phil DeGuere, the executive producer. "John, I don't want you. I think the directors should also produce the shows. The stu-dio is trying to force you down my throat."

"I don't want to be forced down anyone's throat."

So much for that.

I'm around Universal filling in here and there. I get a phone call from Earl Bellamy telling me that *Simon & Simon* is definitely going.

"They're going to do twelve shows. I told Phil DeGuere that he had to use you."

"Earl, I'd be happy to do *Simon & Simon*, but the only way I know how to work is if I have control of certain things. If Phil and I can work it out, fine, otherwise, no way."

"Great, that's why we have you here. That's why we picked up your contract. Just go down and tell him the way it's going to be. Phil has done a number of pilots at Universal. They've gone way over schedule and over budget, and worse than that, none of them sold."

I go down to meet with Phil DeGuere again, feeling a little un-comfortable. There are two other people with him, Richard Chap-man, a producer, and Karen Harris, another producer. Karen is the sister of Bob Harris, the head of Universal TV. I put down my "man-ifesto." I tell Phil exactly what I would do, what he would do, etc. Everybody is stunned. Phil's secretary apparently had her ear to the door because as I open the door to leave, she nearly falls into Phil's office.

The three of them agree to try it out. The only thing that bothers them is my insistence upon hiring the directors. Phil prevails on one point. He wants his director, Alan Levi, to direct shows one and three. I meet with Alan Levi, and Alan tells me all about Alan.

"My nickname at Universal is 'Captain Midnight.'"

"That's nice, Alan. There'll be no 'Captain Midnight' around here. If you want, you can be 'Captain Seven O'Clock.' We'll go over the locations; we'll go over every single day's work. If you find any day that you feel can't be shot in the allotted time schedule, come to me and we'll go to Phil. I don't care what you've done in the past, but on *Simon & Simon*, we have a seven-day schedule. We'll never go over those seven days."

We meet with Phil and go over things. Phil agrees to all the production points. When Alan asks questions, Phil explains, "This is not a documentary, this is a lark!"

Those words rather shocked Alan, but we got through the first show in seven days exactly as scheduled. Everyone, including the studio, was stunned. I think Alan was the most stunned. Alan also did the third show on schedule. Then we brought in other directors. We always gave the directors two shows at a time. One and three, two and four, etc.

One of the directors I brought in was Vince McEveety, not only because he was a great episodic director, but also because I felt I owed him after the *Wonder Woman* fiasco. Once the ball got rolling, it just never stopped. I enjoyed the first twelve shows. *Simon & Simon* was a lot of fun and was the only show I had ever done that I knew my kids, who were now in college, would really like. The way the humor went was "If John understands the joke, take it out. If John doesn't understand the joke, leave it in."

Karen Harris dropped out after the fourth episode. Phil was the guiding force behind the entire show. But it was Richard Chapman who really put the humor into it. Richard, along with writing a number of the scripts, "Simonized" them. He really brought the characters alive. He was funny, witty, and had a complete grasp of the show. He was a brilliant man and great to work with.

Jameson Parker was originally hired to play the part of Rick and happily turned it down to play A. J., who was the more intelligent, straitlaced brother. Finally they found Gerald McRaney to play Rick. Rick was the ne'er-do-well brother, the lovable loser. Although in the beginning the stories focused more on A. J., the fans always rooted for Rick. Rick was more fun for the writers, too. As time went on, Rick's parts got bigger, and the show began to tilt in his favor.

The studio gave us a very limited amount of money in the first year. They never thought the show would make it. Actually, the first year proved them right. We got very low ratings. Even though we got good reviews, people weren't watching.

What we did was take the money we were given and make the show look like an underground movie. We shot on the backlot often, and we did all the stuff in San Diego second unit. We developed a cult following. During the preproduction stage we came up with a rather good idea. We always had script "read-thrus" about seven days before the shows would start filming. At this point, listening to the words being read by the cast, any major problems that the actors or writers might have with the script would be brought up and taken care of. Therefore, discussions on the set would be limited to minor issues. There were no holdups on the set.

We sailed through the first season and then were dropped. However, a show was needed for summer reruns to follow *Magnum P.I.*, which was a huge hit. CBS had tried a couple of shows. They had all failed. Someone suggested *Simon & Simon*. No one had ever watched it, but who knows? We got our chance. In the summer reruns, we took off like a rocket. We were in the top ten. Based upon this, CBS decided to give us thirteen shows for the next season to see how we could do. As it turned out, *Simon & Simon* stayed on the air from 1981 through 1988.

By the time CBS gave us our second chance, we had already dismantled the sets. We had to change everything around and move our offices. I can't resist mentioning the thing that changed in *Simon* the most radically. In season one, clients would come into Rick and A. J.'s office and when they were asked why they had come, the answer would be, "Because we know you're cheap."

When the show became a huge success in season two, the dialogue changed to "Because we hear you're the best."

SIMON SEASON TWO:
WHERE THE CHEAPEST BECOME THE BEST

*R*ick and A. J. got bigger and better offices along with a secretary. The brothers went from lovable losers to constant winners. In the first season Rick would always get beaten up in fights; A. J. couldn't shoot straight and would always miss the target he was aiming at. In the second season, they became so professional they never lost a fight, never made a mistake, and always found the bad guys. The whole charm of season one was lost. It would be like Rockford moving from his trailer into a bungalow at the Beverly Hills Hotel.

At the start of season two, someone at Universal got the brilliant idea to tie the show in with *Magnum P.I.* and have a two-hour opener, with *Magnum P.I.* being the first hour and *Simon & Simon* the second. It was great for us. The *Magnum P.I.* advertisement in *TV Guide* listed their cast with Morgan Fairchild guest starring, along with guest stars Jameson Parker and Gerald McRaney. Who were they? The second hour was billed as *Simon & Simon,* guest starring Tom Selleck, Morgan Fairchild, and John Hillerman. *Magnum P.I.* was number three in the Nielsen ratings for that week. *Simon & Simon* was number two. Don Bellisario, the producer of *Magnum P.I.,* became furious, saying his show had been exploited. He and Phil DeGuere had been good friends, but they didn't speak for three years after that. (Eventually, Phil produced *JAG* for Don Bellisario.)

In the second season and every season thereafter, *Simon & Simon* was a big hit. We were always in the Nielsen top ten, and a lot of times we were number one.

I always had the reputation of hiring people who could get me football or baseball tickets. Notre Dame was coming to Los Angeles to play USC. I remembered a fellow I had used in the past, Tony Longo, who had played for Notre Dame. He was an all-American, and I had hired him a few times to play a gangster. I needed tickets to the game, but I didn't have anything I could use Tony in. Thinking quickly, I realized that on the upcoming episode of *Simon,* with John Astin as our guest star, we were going to be on an island, and we needed someone to play a native chief. I conned everybody into hiring Tony Longo. Of course, no one realized why I wanted him or to what lengths I'd go to get tickets to the Notre Dame game.

We're doing a rehearsal. John Astin is doing a scene with Tony Longo. John can't believe his ears. He hears this thick Philadelphia accent from this character who's supposedly a native chief. John just looks at him and nods during rehearsal. We do the take, and I'll never forget John Astin's famous unscripted line, after Tony has given his speech.

"By the way, what high school did you go to again?"

I was hoping that wouldn't show up in the dailies, but of course it did. Tony wound up sitting on the cutting room floor. I wound up sitting on the fifty-yard line for the Notre Dame game.

Everything was going fine with Phil DeGuere until season four. We were in Paris, and Phil just lost it. He was having problems negotiating his contract with Universal. He had a lot of other tempting offers. He and his agent wound up blowing the Universal deal over $10,000. He agreed to stay on and produce *Simon & Simon* through the end of season four, but he also took a development deal at Disney to produce the new *Twilight Zone* series for CBS. Added to that, he had a development deal with some other place I wasn't familiar with. Simply stated, too much.

What an experience to be in Paris with Phil. You have no idea what it's like to go into a five-star restaurant in Paris with a man who is on a diet. Phil hands the waiter a container of chocolate stuff. "Here. Mix this up for me. This is what I'm having." We all order. Phil then decides to have a little bite of everybody's meal and a little sip of everybody's wine.

Sunday morning arrives, and Phil wants me to come over to his apartment. "John, what I want you to do is sign this deal. I have it all set. All you have to do is fill in the salary and sign."

"What deal? What salary?"

"I've told CBS that we're coming over there to do *Twilight Zone*. They're very excited that you're coming with me."

"Phil, I'm under contract to Universal. I can't do that."

I found out later, speaking with Bob Norvet at CBS, that one of the reasons they wanted Phil, other than for his creative ability, was that I'd be there to keep him in line. Phil had guaranteed that.

After wrapping up in Paris, the *Simon* cast and crew came home. Phil decided that he would stay there and complete the postproduction in Paris. He never returned to Universal. Richard Chapman and I wound up finishing the season as co-executive producers.

THE STARS BECOME *STARS*

*T*o sum up Gerald McRaney, I knew him when he *thought* he knew everything. By the time he got into the third season of *Simon*, he *knew* he knew everything. I mean everything! Gerald knew his character better than anyone did, which in a way is true because once you've worked on a series for three years, you certainly know more about your character than the directors do. I was the only person who knew Gerald and called him Gerald. Everyone else, including his wife, called him Mackey.

Gerald would go into these temperamental tantrums when he wasn't happy with an upcoming scene we were going to do. "Wait a minute. This isn't the way the set was supposed to be."

"Yes it is, Gerald, and besides, you don't have final approval on set dressing."

"I can't work in this set. You have to change this, this, this, and that. I'll be in my dressing room. Let me know when you're ready."

We still got through every show in seven days.

One day we're shooting a scene. Gerald is acting. "Stop! Wait a minute! Where's my canteen?"

"Your canteen?"

"Yes, in order to be doing this scene, we're out here in the woods, and I should have my canteen."

"Okay, fine." The prop man comes up with a canteen.

"No, no, no. This is the wrong canteen. There's a canteen that would be the right canteen for this scene. Go over to my house and get it and bring it back here. Then we can shoot the scene."

We wait around for about an hour. The canteen arrives. "Can we continue now, Gerald?"

I'll never forget Gerald McRaney's last deal with the studio for season seven. I'm on vacation. Ed Masket at the Universal business office calls me at home. "We've made a deal with McRaney. Do you want me to run it by you?"

"Is the deal signed?"

"Yes."

"Okay, Ed, I'm sitting down, tell me the deal."

"We gave McRaney an executive producer credit and final okay on all directors, guest stars, locations, and scripts."

"That sounds wonderful, Ed. I guess we'll do the shows in forty-five days rather then seven."

After completing the second show, Gerald says to me, "John, that director you hired to do the next show? I don't much care for him. You didn't check with me!"

"Gerald, if you want me to check with you, I'll tell you what, you just take over the whole show and produce it. I'm out of here." That was the last time Gerald questioned me with his new deal.

Like all actors, Gerald wanted to direct. We let him direct a couple of *Simon & Simon* shows, but he fell into the trap most actors do. Instead of using their strength, working with actors, they try to show everyone that they know the camera, and they forget the actors.

Gerald's favorite camera move was to put the camera on a dolly for the master shot. He would dolly, following two people until they got into a seated position on the couch. At this point, instead of bringing the camera to a stopping point and finishing the scene, Gerald would keep dollying and dollying until the audience started to wonder if some murderer were going to come in and shoot the people on the couch. We'd try to explain to Gerald that it would be difficult to do coverage on a master shot like that. He'd never listen. He really never listened to anything we ever told him.

Jameson Parker had different opportunities. Jameson was a brooder. He was never, ever, ever on time. He had no idea what time was. He would get in at 9:30 a.m. for an 8:00 a.m. call, put on his bathrobe, and walk onto the set. "Okay, I'm here."

Then he and Gerald would proceed to change the whole scene around even though we'd set it up the night before. We'd have to relight the whole set. The boys would go off to have breakfast. Then they'd go in for makeup and finally get back to the set at 10:30 a.m. We'd already be two-and-a-half hours behind. This was an everyday occurrence when they were in the first scene.

As they were walking onto the set, there'd be a phone call for one of them. Usually Jameson. At that point Jameson only had one ex-wife. It would be his ex-wife's lawyer on the phone, or his business manager, or there was some problem at home. He'd turn around and go back to his dressing room to take the call. Then he'd call his wife at the time, Bonnie, and explain the whole situation to her. By now it's getting close to eleven o'clock. Once Gerald would see that Jameson wasn't on the set, naturally he would leave. Remind you of Sebastian and Brian? This would happen constantly. Finally we'd start shooting. We'd go through everything, quick, quick, and quicker. At 5:30 p.m., Jameson would turn around to me and say, "John, why are we so disorganized? Why are we still here?"

"Jameson, why don't you try coming in at eight o'clock some morning, when your call is?"

"Well, well, I . . . I do that, don't I?"

"No, Jameson, you don't!"

"Well, I try."

"Sure you do."

Another typical day with Jameson. Bonnie would call me on the phone. "John, Jameson is very unhappy with the way work went yesterday. He came home exhausted, and he can't come in this morning. You'd better shoot around him."

I knew what that meant. The good news was that Jameson only lived about three miles from the studio. The bad news was that I would have to go to his house while the set shut down. Thank goodness for Tim Reid, who played Lieutenant "Downtown" Brown on the show. On many occasions Tim saved our lives. He was always there, always prepared, always ready to shoot.

I'd go down to the Parkers' house and have a long talk with them. Jameson loved this. "Okay, let's go."

"You know Jameson, when you finish work tonight, maybe you'd be a little less tired if instead of going to the gym and boxing for an hour and a half, you try going home, having a light supper, and going to bed."

"Oh, I could never do that. I have to go to the gym and work out."

THE *ENQUIRER* CATCHES UP WITH *SIMON & SIMON*

𝓑efore the start of season five, I receive a phone call I'll never forget.

"John, this is William Smitty from the BBC in London. I know you're on hiatus and I've heard you have the best crew in Hollywood. Please send me your crew list. I want to hire them for a documentary I'm doing."

"Look, Mr. Smitty, why don't you call Universal production? I'm sure they'll send you a list. I just don't do that."

"All right."

Somehow, I just didn't trust that call. A few days later, my phone rings. It's our assistant prop master, Bob Silver. "John, I just got a call from some fellow called William Smith of the *National Enquirer*."

"What?"

"Yes. He offered me $2,000 in cash for any juicy story that I could tell him about *Simon & Simon*."

"Did he give you a phone number?"

"Yes."

Bob gives me the number. I dial it. A man answers, and I realize that it's the fellow who passed himself off as William Smitty with an

English accent. Now it's William Smith without the accent. I ask him just what he's trying to do. He's honest about it.

"Look, we have a job to do. Your show's been in the top ten for a number of years now, and it's the only show we have no dirt on. There's nothing on your actors at all. We've got to find something out about them, and I'm trying. I've offered people $2,000 to $3,000, and every one of them has said, 'No, we have nothing to say and if we did it would have to go through John Stephens.'"

"Well, that's complimentary to me, but there is nothing really to talk about concerning the guys. They're married, they live normal lives, and there's nothing unusual at all."

"Can't you give me anything about them? Can you set up an interview for me?"

"An interview? To talk about what? I'll tell you what I'll do. I'll set up an interview for you, with both of them."

"Great."

"However, here's what I want you to do. I'll be back in my office in a week. I want you to send me some stories that you've published in the *Enquirer* that don't rip people apart sexually, or spiritually, or in any way; just nice, honest, clean stories."

"Oh, well, you mean like one of your stars gives ninety percent of their salary to charity?"

"I doubt if they do that, but send me something positive. I don't want any sex stories or anything like that. I'll take it to the guys, and I promise you you'll have an interview." I figure that will be the end of that.

I get back to my office a week later, and there's all this stuff from the *Enquirer* on my desk. I go down to the set before I look at the material. I tell the guys what I've set up, and they're furious. They start calling me names that even Brian Keith had never used.

"Just let me read the stuff, guys."

I read the stuff and find out that the *Enquirer's* idea of being positive is "I had an affair with an alien." "An alien abducted me." I go back down to the set and assure the guys that I'm going to call William Smith and tell him no dice.

I make the call. "Bill, there's no interview."

"Well, we're going to get you, John; one way or the other we'll get you."

"Fine, get us. We're here. Whatever you find out, it had better be true. Go ahead and get us."

About three months later, Smith calls again. "John, we at the *Enquirer* have the same rules other publications have. Before we publish a story on somebody, we have to inform the company or the persons themselves about the story and what we're going to publish."

"Fine, let me hear what you've got."

"Well, John, we happen to know that one of your stars is dying."

"Really, that's interesting, why don't you tell me which one it is and then we'll both know."

"You know who it is, John. It's Jameson Parker."

"Jameson Parker? Okay, what's he dying of?"

"He has a very bad back. We have all the medical reports on him, and at the most he has three months to live. You know that and I know that, and we're going to publish it."

"I'll tell you what Bill. Why don't you publish it, and I'll be glad to show you something a little better than any doctor's report you could come up with, which veracity I'll certainly doubt. Jameson, like a lot of people in America, has a back problem. It's hardly chronic. He does see a doctor. He occasionally has a chiropractor come in and work on his back. Millions of Americans have this problem. Are they all dying? I'll show you every production report for every day that Jameson has worked. He's never missed a day's work in his life because of any back problems. Not only that, I'll even show you a list of all the stunts he has done himself that I doubt any man who's dying could do. On our last two episodes he did his own running at UCLA. This included running hurdles, which very few stunt men can do. He's dying from back problems? Good luck. And good luck to you and the *Enquirer*."

I go down to the set and tell Jameson the whole story. He has a fit.

"Oh no, he's going to publish it. How could you be so stupid? I'll call my lawyer—"

"Don't do anything. Believe me, they won't publish it."

They never did.

THE STARS STRIKE BACK

*G*erald and Jameson, of all the new stars, were certainly the best. Sure they had a lot of faults, things I wasn't used to. They knew more than anyone else knew, and they didn't respect authority, except their own, but if you were honest with them, they gave you their best. Once they trusted you, you could do no wrong.

Before the start of season three, we had a salary dispute. When they first signed Jameson and Gerald, Jameson was supposed to be the star of the show. He was coming off a starring role in a soap opera, and Gerald had only done small character parts. So when they were hired, their salaries were considerably apart. I'd say, to the best of my knowledge, they were about $15,000 to $20,000 per episode apart. Before the start of season three, because it was *Simon & Simon* and because they were good friends, Jameson and Gerald decided that their salaries should be equal. If this didn't happen, they would go on strike.

The whole thing went back and forth. The studio was yelling and screaming, the network was yelling and screaming, and I kind of got into the middle of it. I went to the powers and took the boys' side. "Jameson and Gerald should be equal." Universal said that would be setting a precedent. Universal set and unset more precedents than any studio in Hollywood history.

The boys were speaking to me. They weren't speaking to anybody else. They wouldn't tell me whether they were coming back or not, and the studio wouldn't tell me whether they were going to make a deal with them or not. The situation became difficult. We started in with shooting some second unit footage. There were stunt shots without the stars, and some other scenes without them.

Finally I get a phone call from Michael Karg, Gerald's agent. "The deal has been settled. They got equal salaries with a raise for both. They'll be back at work tomorrow. John, when Mackey comes on the set, I want you to arrange for the whole crew to stand up and cheer."

"Bullshit, Michael! The crew's not going to stand up at all. The crew does their job. They've been here every day. If this'd really been a prolonged thing, the whole crew would've been out of work. They'll treat Gerald and Jameson with the same respect they've always treated them, period. No cheering."

That was that. They came back. All was forgiven.

Gerald and Jameson's feelings about directors were interesting. The only director I ever hired who they were really excited about was Burt Kennedy. He'd done a lot of John Wayne movies. Even Phil DeGuere was excited about getting Burt. "Burt is a filmmaker and I love filmmakers."

Burt was the only director on *Simon & Simon* the boys were in awe of. In filming his first show, whatever Burt said was gospel. The second show that Burt did, whatever Burt said was gospel. The third show, whatever Gerald and Jameson said was gospel! Burt was just another director.

One day Burt turns to Gerald on the set. "Ya know, Mackey, you wouldn't believe this, but I once actually directed a show all by myself without any help from anybody."

This shuts Gerald up for the next two scenes, but by the third scene he's helping Burt direct again. "I wouldn't do this, wouldn't it be better if this, wouldn't it be better if that . . . " Et cetera, et cetera.

The boys liked some of the directors. They loved Vince McEveety. They loved Sig Neufeld. I told all the directors before I hired them that the situation was simple.

"The actors know the show better than you do. You have to listen to what they say, allot time for their suggestions, and incorporate their suggestions. Just make sure that their suggestions never ruin the story."

I made a number of mistakes by never hiring young directors. This happened with Donald Petrie. At the start of his career, Petrie was assigned by Universal to observe *Simon & Simon*. I'd seen a film he'd made at the American Film Institute (AFI), which was brilliant. The AFI is a school for young aspiring Hollywoodites in all areas of the industry. Students get to direct their own short films, many of which are shown to studios and give future directors their start.

After auditing our show, Petrie expected to direct an episode of *Simon & Simon*. I was worried because I felt that he was young and inexperienced, and to give him his first directorial shot, so to speak, would be a disaster. The guys would just walk all over him instead of helping him. I turned him down. Boy, was I wrong. Don went on to direct *Mystic Pizza* and many other big features.

Another director who had done a film at AFI was set to audit *Simon*. Universal asks me to view this fellow's film. The film consists of a turtle crossing the road. Just a turtle, just a road. There's music, sound effects of cars screeching, and twenty minutes of a turtle crossing a road. Of course, as you've guessed, the last shot was the one car that wasn't able to screech around it, and that was the end of the turtle.

When I get back to my office Jim Korris calls me. "Well? Well? What'd ya think of his work? Wasn't it great?"

"Yeah, it was wonderful. Next time we have a show starring a turtle, I'll definitely hire him."

"Now, John, you have to let him do something. He's done one other thing at AFI, let me get that to you."

After the hopeful director audits our show, he comes into my office.

"I'm impressed; I want to direct one of your shows. Let me show you another AFI film I did. I know you weren't impressed by the turtle, but let me show you a film I did with actors. I know you'll love it."

I view the film with him. It's dreadful. We go back to my office, and I tell him, "Well, that really wasn't too good. The actor was overacting, and the actress was in a bad mood when she was supposed to be happy the whole time."

"John, let me explain. The actors were just moody that day, and I couldn't get anything out of them."

"If you can't get anything out of them, what do you think you're going to do dealing with Jameson Parker and Gerald McRaney?"

Needless to say, I didn't hire him either.

I had the complete say on directors. I hire Sig Neufeld to direct a show. I get a call from Phil DeGuere.

"This is the worst director you've ever hired. How could you do this to me? This is awful. He'll ruin the show."

"Look, that's our deal, and I'm going to stand by Sig, I know he's going to do a good job."

"He ruined my best *Black Sheep Squadron*. He's ruined a lot of shows that I've written."

I decide not to go to the dailies. Every day I get a phone call from Phil, who says, "John, these were the worst dailies ever. We'll have to reshoot the whole show. I hope you're happy. This time you've really screwed things up." This goes on for seven days.

Phil calls me two weeks later. "I think you'd better come to the rough cut." The rough cut is the first assemblage of the show after the director has seen it. "I want you to be there to see how awful this episode turned out."

"No way, Phil, I'm not coming."

The phone rings an hour later. "John, I've just seen the rough cut. It's the best rough cut we've ever had."

"Thank you, Phil." Thank you, dear Lord. Sig was in and could do no wrong.

A GOOD SCRIPT TO START THE SEASON

*A*t the beginning of season five, I get a script written by Gerald McRaney's wife, Pat. I read it. It's not too good. The episode has Mary Carver, who played the boys' mother, starring in it as a "sexpot" dance hall girl, like Kitty in *Gunsmoke*. Mary was hardly Amanda Blake.

Pat and Gerald call me about the script every night during our hiatus. "This is where locations should be. Now what do you think of . . ." What do I think about this, what do I think about that.

"Yeah, sure, well, maybe we could just—"

"Now, John, we know you're not a big fan of Mary Carver, but this is going to be the best Western ever done."

"Wait a minute, Gerald—"

"No, John, you wait a minute. This is the best script I've ever read. Pat's written a gem. I'm proud of her. I think this should be the show that we use to kick off the season."

"We can't do that, Gerald. It has to be filmed on location if we do it, and—"

"What do you mean, *if* we do it? We're doing it!"

We get close to where we're starting to make the schedule out and get close to filming. I call up Richard Chapman. This was to be his last year on the show. "Richard, have you read Pat's script?"

"Ah, yeah, I've . . . I've read it."

"It's not good."

"That's being kind."

"Did you tell her that?"

"No. I'm not going to tell her."

"Richard, do you think we're ever gonna do this show?"

"No, of course we're not going to do it! Take care of it, will you?"

"Okay, Richard, I'll tell her."

It's a Friday when Gerald McRaney and his agent, Michael Karg, are in my office discussing the upcoming season. I decide to broach the subject of Pat's script. "Gerald, can I ask you a question?"

"Sure."

"This script that Pat wrote?"

"What about it?"

"Gerald, are you gonna sit there and tell me this is the best script you've ever read?"

"God, no."

"Then why didn't you tell Pat?"

"I don't want to tell her."

"Michael, have you read this script?"

"Yes, I . . . I couldn't believe it."

"Gerald, I'm going to call her up and tell her that we're not going to do the script."

"Why do you always have to be the one that does these things?"

"Mackey's right, you shouldn't have to do that."

"Good. Do either of you guys want to do it?"

"No."

"No."

"Fine, then I'm gonna do it."

Then comes the bombshell. Gerald says, "Now, John, by the way, don't call her over the weekend, call her on Monday."

"I'm going to call her right now."

"No, John, you can't do that."

"Why?"

"Because I'm moving out over the weekend. I'm leaving her."

I called her on Monday. She didn't speak to me for fifteen years. Since then Pat has gone on to become an accomplished screenwriter.

The most difficult part of *Simon & Simon* was dealing with the evening phone calls. It always worked the same way. Here's a typical example. At five o'clock in the afternoon, my assistant, Sally, buzzes me.

"Pat McRaney's on the phone."

"Okay."

"John? Pat!"

"Yes, Pat." (This was before the script incident.)

"You know Mackey's the star of the show."

"Pat, it's called *Simon & Simon*."

"John, we all know that Mackey's the star of the show! Look, his parts have got to get bigger, and more importantly, he should direct five or six shows during the coming season. You know what a fine director he is."

"Sure I do, Pat. Sure, absolutely . . . "

This goes on for about thirty minutes. Next buzz from Sally.

"Bonnie Parker's on the line."

"Yes, Bonnie?"

"John, this show is not *Simon & Simon* anymore. It's Rick Simon's. This show started in with Jameson as the star. Jameson, very nicely, brought Mackey up so they were equals, but now Mackey has shoved Jameson aside. We've got to get this straight. They are equals. If anything, Jameson should be the star of the show. Now do you have that straight?"

"I agree, and I thought it was that way."

"Well, it isn't that way." Bonnie goes on and on.

Then comes the third phone call, which I can happily say, I take at home. It's Phil DeGuere's wife, Linda.

"John, you know I'm doing this part tomorrow. I understand you don't think I'm up to it. You told Phil he should change the dialogue and just give me two lines. Why would you say that and hurt me so? You know what a fine actress I am." I can actually hear Phil on the other line laughing.

"Phil, do you want to get in on the conversation? If you don't, hang up!" I hear the phone click. I'd never know if he'd pick it up again or not.

Linda starts in again. "And John, the gift that you gave to the crew?"

"What about it?"

"Those were awful jackets. We're the number one show in America. I've ordered satin jackets in maroon and gold for the entire crew. Make sure that the studio picks up the charges."

"Sure, Linda, whatever you say."

Linda presented the new jackets to the crew. The studio paid for them. I gave mine to Goodwill.

UNIVERSAL'S SUITS—THE *SIMON* "BIBLE"

I've always felt that the biggest mistake that people make in television is all the time spent working on budgets. Most people don't seem to realize that you film the script; you don't film the budget. If you want to be on budget, change the script. Don't say, "We can cut out two electricians, cut out one grip, cut out three trucks," etc. Remember, what's on the screen is the script, not the budget.

When I first got to Universal, Don Sipes was the head of TV as far as the creative area was concerned. Universal had very few shows at that time. Don was only in that position for one year while I was there. The second year Robert Harris came in. He was great. He let everybody do what they had to do to run the shows as they saw fit. Following Robert Harris, Kerry McCluggage came in.

Kerry and I met on the pilot *Brass Monkey*. He was a hands-on person who wanted to be involved in everything. Kerry left us alone on *Simon & Simon* since we were a successful show. He was an extremely talented person. I think that in any field that you're in, whether it's show biz or anything else, you don't necessarily have to like people to realize they're good at their jobs. I admired Kerry McCluggage a lot. He either brought in or kept many creative producers. He went on to Paramount and had great success there.

One of Kerry's underlings, Gary Hart (no, not that Gary Hart), calls me one day. He says he's new to TV. "John, Universal wants me to audit your show to find out how things are done."

"Okay, that'll be great."

"Send me the schedule. I want to know everything that goes on."

"That's a great idea, Gary, it'll help a lot."

After I send the schedule, I call Gary's secretary to ask if he's received it. "Yes, he has, and he wants to talk to you about it."

"Okay, sure."

Gary comes on the line. "John, you want me in all the preproduction meetings and all, that's fine. On the first day of filming you want me on location at five-thirty in the morning? Are you crazy?!"

"Gary, if you want to really learn the business, I want you to see where the problems occur and where the opportunities occur. When the first trucks arrive, that's when the first opportunities arrive. Certain places are designated for parking. People come out and say, 'No, you can't park here.' Police have their say on different permits that may not be correct. I want you to see how we deal with this and also the actor and director problems."

"John, I'm sure all that is interesting, but I'll be by at about nine-thirty."

"That's fine, Gary, but by that time we'll be filming. By the way, are you going to come back when we wrap?"

"What time will that be?"

"Around 6:00 p.m."

"I haven't got time for that."

I guess Gary didn't need to know about trucks and parking. As of this writing, he is the head of Paramount TV!

Jim Korris, Kerry McCluggage's right-hand man at Universal, calls me one day. Dick Lindheim, another Universal exec, is on the other line. "We've got a great idea for you. We've got this great guest star, you're gonna love it. CBS has okayed the extra money."
"Really, who's that?"
"Joan Rivers."
"Joan Rivers? I'll tell you this, I'm not going to say what I think about Joan Rivers, but I am going to talk to the guys. If they say 'fine,' it's fine with me."
I head down to the stage. The guys go bananas. "If Joan Rivers walks on our set, we'll walk off!"
I relay the information to Korris.
"I'm going to go down there right away and straighten them out."
Joan Rivers never appeared on our show.

One thing that Phil DeGuere and I agreed to do was to make a "bible" for *Simon & Simon*. A "bible" lists all of the characters, all of their backgrounds, where they went to grammar school and high school, their love lives, if they went into the service or didn't go into the service, and every single thing about them. After the "bible" for *Simon* was completed, it was handed to the stars. They had the right to make any changes to the descriptions of their characters. What happens on a number of shows that don't make a "bible"—I learned this working at Fedderson—is that all of a sudden one of the actors will say, "Wait a minute, my character wouldn't do this because he this and he that." No one knows, if it isn't in writing, whether the character did this or did that, so it's really an important thing to have it all written down. Any writer who came on *Simon & Simon* was always given a copy of our "bible."
Before our production meetings, we had preproduction meetings discussing wardrobe, stunts, locations, etc. Our production meetings only lasted forty-five minutes. Anyone in the production meetings who started to question dialogue was immediately stopped. "This is a production meeting, not a script conference."
In the late 1970s, and by the time *Simon* was in production in the 1980s, if somebody wrote a script, and it was bought, that was fine. If

the writer sold a second script, they immediately became a story editor. With their third sold script, they were made a producer; with the fourth, an executive producer. With the fifth they were writing their own ticket. At one time, there were ten producers of *Simon & Simon*, most of whom I never met.

These people were not allowed in production meetings or casting sessions. They weren't allowed to go on the set and discuss anything with the director. They just wrote. When they left Universal, they would say they'd produced *Simon & Simon*. I'd get calls asking about so-and-so saying they'd produced *Simon & Simon*. "No, they didn't."

I find that on sitcoms especially, there's a writer who often only writes for one character, and that person is also called a producer. So much for the term "producer" in television.

THE AGONY AND THE ECSTASY OF LOCATIONS

*T*he locations we used on *Simon & Simon* were numerous. We went to Paris. This was a very tough location. The Parisians didn't know *Simon & Simon*. It wasn't on French TV. The French would tell us one thing, and we'd get it all set up. We'd start to film in the lobby of a hotel. They'd tell us we had until twelve o'clock. At nine o'clock a new manager would come up and say, "You have to be out of here at nine-thirty." It probably would have been a lot easier had we been Angela Lansbury or been doing a cooking show.

San Diego was the best place in the world to work. They loved us there. We were never turned away from any location in San Diego. Las Vegas was tough for me because of my gambling problem. We had a certain guest star who decided to start dating a particular girlfriend of a well-known mobster in Vegas. The mobster came to the set one day and informed me that if there was any more dating by this gentleman of his lady, the gentleman would be found at the bottom of Hoover Dam. I informed the gentleman of that. There was no more dating of the lady.

The most important person when you're going on location is the location manager. We had a number of location managers on *Simon & Simon*. We started with Rick Muhrlein. Rick was divorced from his wife. He had no money and no home. He slept in his car. It was a miracle that he ever got us any locations. Rick had an especially difficult time in getting mansions.

The worst situation that happened with Rick was one time when we needed a bank building. We stopped outside the bank. Rick got out of the car and went into the bank. Luckily the alarms didn't go off. Obviously we weren't allowed to film in the bank.

Rick would always say yes, he had this and yes, he had that, and he'd just hope when he got there, he'd get it. For one episode, we wanted to shoot in a shipyard. Rick shows us one.

"Great, Rick, now do you have it all arranged?"

"Everything is all arranged, everything is fine."

"We're going to be here at six o'clock in the morning."

"Everything is arranged, the gates will be open to you, it's all set."

We get there at six in the morning. Not only is no one there, the gates are clamped tight and there is a lock on them.

"Do we have this location?"

"Well, I think so."

We gamble, which we should have never done, but it works out. One of the crewmembers saws the lock off. We open the gate and start filming. When the guard arrives there, Rick has to make the deal with him.

Another time, we need a ship. We go down to this pier and see the perfect ship. "This is going to be great! Thanks, Rick, good job. We're shooting this next week."

The next week comes. We get there, no ship.

"I forgot to tell the people. I didn't think you'd be here today."

"It's on the schedule, Rick and you know we've always stuck to the schedule."

We changed the script and used a salvage yard nearby.

The location manager who followed Rick was Paul Brinkman. He was the son of the actress Jeanne Crain and Paul Brinkman Sr. My assistant, Sally, was all excited.

"I can't wait to meet him, he's gotta be so good-looking . . ."

"Sally, we're hiring him as a location manager, not as an actor."

We have to shoot an episode just north of the Mexican border on the American side. It's a very tough show with a lot of action. Paul shows us this place that's ideal. We take the director down there and work out all the action.

"Paul, you couldn't have done a better job." Paul is beaming.

The Friday before Labor Day, our production manager, Jim Gardner, calls me up. "Paul and I have to come up to discuss something with you. That location in San Diego that we love so much? I think we have a problem."

"Come on up."

"We're on our way."

A while later, Paul and Jim walk into my office. "Paul, why don't you tell John what's happening."

"Well, there's a slight problem with the fellow who owns the property. He says we can't film on it."

"Well, Paul, that's more than a slight problem."

"No, no, John here's the good news. The owner of the property is a Catholic."

"Oh?"

"I've talked with his priest."

"And?"

"His priest is going to get in touch with him and try to talk him into it. I'm sure he'll listen to his priest."

"Wait a minute, Paul. You didn't mention to John that the owner has sold the property, and it's in escrow. He's not going to take any chances of something happening to the property."

"I didn't tell you that, John, should I have?"

"I'll tell you what, Paul, we're going back down to San Diego on Sunday with the director. You get down there right away and find us two or three other locations that will work out."

Paul did find us a location. It was not as good as the first one.

In another situation with Paul, we're looking for a doughnut shop where Rick and A. J. will stop to get doughnuts, then be on their way. Vince McEveety is directing the show. Paul takes us out to a place in Glendale and shows us a window.

"Okay, where's the doughnut shop?"

"This is the doughnut shop here."

"I don't understand. This is just a piece of glass, it's a window. There's nothing behind it but a vacant building."

"Well, I thought you could, in cuts, have Mackey out in front of the glass. Then not see what's behind him and then have him walk towards the car and give Jameson the doughnuts."

"I'll tell you what, Paul. Why don't you explain it to Mackey? Meanwhile we'll be looking for another location."

Another time we're going to shoot a location near the studio. All we need is a house with a porch. A. J. and Rick will go to the porch and knock on the door. An elderly lady will answer the door and say, "Yes, I have information on that person. Why don't you come into the backyard and have some iced tea with me? I'll be trimming some roses, if you don't mind." That's the scene. It's vital that we have a porch and that the actors can go into the backyard. That's the whole idea of the scene.

The street Paul takes us to has at least ten houses with porches. Basically, every house in that area has a little porch on it where you open the front door. You know the rest. Paul takes us to the one house that doesn't have a porch. "Why are we going here?"

"Well, this lady is so friendly, I thought you'd like to shoot here. She's got a backyard. There's no table nor roses, but I thought you could rewrite the script for that."

"Paul, that's fine. Let's find a house with a porch. Maybe the people won't be so friendly, but maybe they'll have a backyard with a table and some roses. Also, Paul, the people who own the house are not in the show."

We all do things like this when we start out. Paul later became the location manager for *JAG*.

One night back in 1981, after I had completed the first thirteen episodes of *Simon & Simon*, my wife and I were watching TV and there was an advertisement for a new Universal show called *The Gangster Chronicles*.

"Why can't you get on a show like that?"

"I don't know."

Soon afterwards I got a phone call asking me to go up to the office of Gerry Gottleib, Universal's head of Business Affairs.

LUCKY LUCIANO: "A TRUE AMERICAN HERO"

*G*erry says, "We're making some changes on *Gangster Chronicles*. We've done the first three shows. We don't like the way they went. We're letting the director, Richard Sarafian, go and we're bringing in a whole new team of people."

I'm introduced to Matt Rapf and his assistant, Mark Rodgers. I have no idea why they're there or why I'm there. Gerry says, "Guys, this show is a disaster. We're going to make it into an episodic show. We have ten more shows to do, and they're all going to be episodic.

"John Stephens is in charge of everything. Nothing gets done unless John agrees with it, everybody understand that?" I'm thinking to myself, here I am again, back to Peter Tewksbury at Don Fedderson.

Gerry continues, "Matt, you're the executive producer. Mark, you're the producer. But you have to clear everything with John."

The door opens, and Jim McAdams walks in. "This is Jim McAdams. He's the supervising producer of the show."

This had all the makings of a gigantic mess.

A number of things went wrong with *Gangster Chronicles*. Nothing went right, starting with the idea. For some reason Hollywood's always been in love with gangsters and the mob. I've never been in love with gangsters or the mob.

The people from Universal, along with Richard Alan Simmons, a very talented writer, had gone down to Florida and met with Meyer Lansky. Obviously, they'd believed everything Lansky had told them about the good old days when the Mafia ruled the world. They had come back and put together a show where the "hero" was Lucky Luciano. The other two heroes were Meyer Lansky, going by the name of Michael Lasker, and Bugsy Siegel. The bad guy in the show was Dutch Schultz. Dutch Shultz was in fact a bad guy, but the others were hardly heroes. We had lines in the script with Luciano saying things like "We never deal in drugs!" Most people know that Lucky Luciano was one of the main kingpins bringing drugs into the U.S. Al Capone was another one of our heroes. *Gangster Chronicles* is the only show that I ever did that I was embarrassed about doing.

Richard Sarafian was told that he was being fired just as he was finishing postproduction on the third episode. Sarafian calls the actors in. What a cast: Michael Nouri, Joe Penny, and Brian Benben were the three principals. Jonathan Banks played Dutch Schultz.

Sarafian says, "Listen, just remember you're the stars, don't ever come onto the set unless you feel you're ready. If you feel a scene is wrong, go back to your dressing room, think things through. Don't let them rush you. They're going to try to rush you; don't let them! We've established this show together. Don't worry about the time. Universal has all the time in the world, and they have all the money in the world. This is your show, so don't let them take it away from you." How would you like to follow that kind of speech?

In all fairness to the actors, as awful as I thought they were, and as awful as they thought I was, there was never any attempt to explain to them what was going on. We were never allowed to get in a room and discuss things. We were just thrust upon them. Sarafian was gone, and there we were.

We started doing episode four. Sarafian was gone but, as the song goes, "His memory lingered on." We had a director who'd already been hired to do two shows, Leo Penn, whose main claim to fame was that he was Sean Penn's father. He'd done a lot of good things in his day, but he had another one of those drinking problems. We finally got rid of him. I brought in my own directors and basically my own crew to try to get things worked out.

The actors were really something. Michael Nouri played Lucky Luciano. The day would normally start with Michael coming in. He'd scream obscenities, pick up a chair, and break various things in his motor home. The last thing he would break would be the window in his motor home. Then he'd storm off.

Joe Penny, who played Bugsy Siegel, would come in and outdo Michael with his yelling of obscenities. He'd go onto the set and break something. For instance, we'd be set up to film in a bar. Joe would go by, pick up a bar stool and throw it against the back bar, breaking all the glasses. Then he'd storm off the set.

Brian Benben, who played the mastermind of the group, Michael Lasker (Meyer Lansky), was a little bit more gentle. Brian would phone each morning. "John, this is Brian."

"I know, Brian, your back is bothering you."

"How did you know, John?"

"I could tell last night."

"You could? You could tell I was in real pain, right?"

"Yes, Brian."

Brian wouldn't be in that day. He actually was the least of the problems.

Jim McAdams, the supervising producer, had a girlfriend at the time who he thought was a great actress and singer. She was always given big parts. McAdams's girlfriend is going to sing a song in one of the shows, so Jim hires a studio for the weekend. "John, Joy is going to rehearse her songs."

"Whatever you say, Jim, that's fine."

"You know she's got a real big scene to do on Monday morning before she sings. I'm going to have Leo go over her lines with her." Leo Penn was directing. This was his last show.

Jim goes on. "Michael has agreed to go over there, too. Make sure they're paid for the day."

"That's fine, as long as we get it."

They work and work. Sunday night Jim calls me. "Everything's going to be great! Boy, is it gonna be perfect. Thanks for okaying the studio."

"No problem, Jim."

We get in Monday morning. The first thing we do is rehearse the scene. We rehearse the scene from eight-thirty to eleven-thirty. Leo asks me to come down to the set.

"John, she can't do the scene."

"She can't do the scene? What do you mean she can't do the scene?"

"She's not up to it. She needs at least another week of prep on this scene."

"That's nice."

"She's so upset that she can't do the scene that she's left for the day. I thought you'd like to know that. So, no song either."

"Leo, that's just great."

We decide to rehearse a scene for the next day that we know we can shoot with Joe Penny. By this time Joe is upset with everything and everybody. A dropped hat would upset Joe. He finally agrees to start rehearsing the scene.

We have an elderly grip [stagehand] on the show. He's up on a ladder putting up a scrim [a scrim is a type of theater drop] for one of the lights. There's another ladder right next to where he's working. As Joe's rehearsing, he's getting madder and madder. All of a sudden he says those famous Brian Keith words, "Fuck this!" He kicks the ladder that's in front of him. The ladder crashes into the grip's ladder and the grip falls off. We call an ambulance and send him to the hospital. Joe Penny walks off the set. Doesn't even look back. Couldn't care less. Luckily it wasn't a serious injury.

Jonathan Banks was great. Markie Post, who played Jonathan's girlfriend, was also great.

"Boy, you guys have saved us so many times. I'll never forget you. Is it hard acting with these jerks?"

"It's easy. I'm supposed to hate these guys, and it's a cinch to hate them."

GANGSTER CHRONICLES GOES DOWN

If you think the three stars of the show were terrible, they were nothing compared to Robert Davi. He kept trying to outdo those three in bad behavior. Robert has become a semi-star. He has a great face. It's pockmarked and very interesting. Occasionally he plays lead detectives and has been in a television series, *The Profiler.* He is a very good actor, but his actions on *Gangster Chronicles* were unbelievable.

Robert goes through the first seven episodes. Then one day I get a call to come down to makeup right away. The makeup artist points to Robert. He has makeup covering up all the pits in his face.

"Robert, what is this?"

"Well, I thought I'd have a new look."

"Robert, the episode that we're in now, we've already shot half of you with your other look. We don't shoot in continuity, as you know, so how the devil is this gonna match?"

"That doesn't make any difference, John, I'm going ahead with my new look."

"Robert, either take that makeup off and go back to your normal look, or we'll write you out of the episode and maybe the rest of the series."

For the first time, an actor on *Gangster Chronicles* listened to me.

Michael Nouri would have scenes with Robert Davi. Davi would always throw something extra in. Say there's a line like "You got back from Rome, how was it?"

Davi is supposed to reply, "Italy's fine." That's the line, but Robert would always add something extra.

"Italy is fine, you can't believe all the great things that Mussolini is doing. The trains are running on time, the food is great . . . " Etc., etc.

I go up to him after one of the shows. "Robert, why are you adding all this dialogue?"

"Well, I thought it was interesting."

"We're not going to use it."

"Well, it was interesting anyway."

We're down to the final days of *Gangster Chronicles*. We're doing a scene where there's a big meeting during which the gangsters are all discussing the Democratic Convention. A henchman runs into the room and says to Lucky, "Lucky, Lucky, good news! You've just been elected to be a delegate to the Democratic Convention, and that means we're going to get our man Roosevelt in."

"That's great!"

I finally blow my top. I'm not going to discuss my political affiliation except to say this. I know that a man who was not even a citizen of the United States is not about to be the delegate from New York at the Democratic Convention. It so happened there was a fellow named Kellem DeForrest who handled everything in research. He had a library. I get the book that lists all the delegates to the Democratic Convention in 1932. Obviously there is no Lucky Luciano on the list.

I bring this to Matt Rapf's attention. "I've really taken enough of this with the glorifying gangsters and all of that. I accepted Tom Dewey sitting in a bar having a drink with Lucky Luciano. But this is the end. This is absolutely unbelievable."

"Okay, we're going to make you happy."

They don't give me the revisions until the day we're shooting the scene. What's the big change?

"Good news, Lucky, you're an alternate!"

Which wasn't true either, of course. I'm thinking, okay, it's the last day, so let's get on with it. But the day isn't over yet. Robert Davi comes to me.

"John, we're all sitting around in this hotel room, waiting to hear that Roosevelt's gonna be nominated. We know that Roosevelt is not gonna ever put through this deal of repealing Prohibition; that's why we're all for him." That part was true. "I'm sitting there and I have nothing to do. What do you suggest I do?"

"Robert, why don't you get yourself a toenail clipper, take off your shoes and socks, and be clipping your toenails while everybody else is talking. I think that would be a brilliant move."

Fortunately, he decided not to take my suggestion.

Susan Lloyd played Joe Penny's wife. She went along with everything the trio did. Later, any time any of their names would come up in casting, I'd say, "No way! No way! *Never!*" Susan Lloyd's name comes up, and I give the same answer. Our casting director, Donna Dockstader, says, "John, why don't you meet her and hear her side of the story?"

"No, no, she's terrible, terrible."

Donna keeps after me. "Okay, I'll meet her."

Susan Lloyd comes in.

"John, look. I was in a situation while working with those guys and playing Joe Penny's wife. I can't start taking the side of production or getting in fights or arguments with Joe or Michael or tell them to start acting professional. Nothing would have gotten done."

"Susan, you're absolutely right."

Happily I was able to work with Susan a couple of times on other shows. She was great, no problem. That's a mistake that you can make. Find out the whole story before you rush to make a judgment about someone.

Back to *Simon & Simon*. One day in 1983, Phil DeGuere calls me into his office.

"I've got a great idea. You're going to love it!"

COMPUTERS, COREY, AND MAX GAIL'S PONYTAIL

*P*hil says, "Bob Shane and I have created a series, and we're going to do a pilot. It's called *Whiz Kids*. It's all local locations. It's about a bunch of computer whizzes. We want you to produce the show and for the director, I want Burt Kennedy."

"What?"

"I love Burt Kennedy. He's a filmmaker, I told you that. I've got to have Burt Kennedy direct this pilot."

"Phil, I know Burt very well. I know the way pilots are done on this lot. You're gonna be on the set every minute of every day, and Burt Kennedy is not going to put up with that."

"No, no, I . . . I won't bother him at all."

"I'll tell you what, Phil, I'll call him and then I want to have a meeting with the two of you."

"Fine, fine, bring him in, bring him in."

Burt comes in, excited about doing a pilot. It's a different type of show for him: kids solving crimes with the help of a friendly computer. Burt figures it will be good for his career, which was in limbo at the time.

"Burt, I want you to know this. Phil will be on the set every minute and after every shot, he's going to tell you whether he liked it or not."

Burt doesn't believe me. "That's fine with me, John. Phil, that'll be fine. We'll work great together. Don't worry about a thing."

We have a day of rehearsal on the stage just to walk through the script for blocking. Everybody has a headset on. It's the same as doing a three-camera show. I'm up in the booth with Phil. Burt is on the floor directing the actors. We get ready for the first rehearsal. Burt runs everybody through the scene.

Phil's watching and listening on a monitor up in the booth. He has his headset on, and he's listening to the dialogue. The scene finishes. Phil rips off his headset and, not caring that the mike is open on the stage, says, "What in the hell was that? That was total shit. That was the worst-directed scene ever."

"John, get down here!"

I go down to the stage, knowing full well what's going to happen. Burt takes off his headphones and throws them on the floor.

"I don't need this. I quit!"

"Burt, I warned you."

But Burt, like Elvis, had "left the building."

Phil gets another idea. "I want Corey Allen."

"No way are you going to have Corey Allen. Remember our deal, Phil, I can have a 'ding' on the director, and I have five dings on Corey Allen."

Phil goes to the studio. The studio pleads with me. They finally tell Phil, "If John's not going to okay him, we're not going to okay him."

It finally comes down to a meeting with Corey Allen. I had never met Corey in person before, but his reputation preceded him. He had the reputation of thinking there were no such things as hours, no such things as days, and no such thing as a schedule. The day he comes in for our meeting, he's wearing an outfit that wound up becoming very familiar. I don't think he had any other outfits. It consists of an old yellow sweater, baggy Levis, torn tennis shoes, and no socks. As John Mantley would say, "He's the most scrofulous person I've ever seen."

Corey promises me he'll do the show on time. Just give him a chance. I can be there every second of the day. I agree to give him a chance. We do the pilot and, miracle of miracles, Corey actually gets the show done going only half a day over schedule, a delay which was due to illness.

The show was turned into a series, and the network comes up with a cast change. They want Max Gail for the newspaper reporter. Max was brilliant on *Barney Miller* playing the Polish detective. Three days before filming, I'm called in to meet Max Gail.

"Nice to meet you, Max."

"Phil, I've gotta leave. See you later, John, look forward to working with you."

He walks out the door. I turn to Phil. "Phil, does the network know about Max's appearance?"

"What do you mean?"

"Phil, this guy is supposed to be playing a respected newspaper reporter. He looks like a hippie and what little hair he has is done up in a ponytail. It's okay with me if the network knows this. Phil, do they know it?"

"Honestly?"

"Yes, Phil, honestly."

"No."

"Don't you think you should tell them what to expect? When they see the first day's dailies, they're going to faint."

"No, no, John, they're gonna love it."

"Phil, you're taking a chance."

"Don't worry, everything will be fine."

The first day we're filming, I ask Max about the ponytail. "What's wrong with the ponytail? This ponytail stays with me. That's the only reason I took this job. I've been turned down for a number of other jobs because of the way I look. This is me, this is the way I am, and this is the way it's gonna be, get it?"

"Yeah, Max, I've got it."

The next day the network gets the dailies before we do. Phil calls me into his office.

"John, the network has just seen the dailies for the *Whiz Kids*. We've got a problem."

"Gee, Phil, what's that?"

"They want Max to remove his ponytail."

"Oh? Well, I guess you're going to tell him."

"No, John, you tell him."

"Phil."

"John, that's your job, you tell him."

"Okay."

I go out to location and tell Max. "The network insists on a haircut, or they're not going to let the show go on with you in the role."

"They don't have any right to–"

"Max, that's what they're insisting on."

"Well, you come in here tomorrow morning, and you and I are going to agree on how short it's going to be."

"Fine, Max."

I get in at 6:30 a.m. and Max and I go back and forth. No, one more hair; no, two more hairs; three more hairs, etc. What we wind up with is a rather unkempt look to say the least. The ponytail is gone, but the rest of his hair defies description.

Max decides he wants to direct a show. His directorial debut is less than brilliant. We have a huge action scene at the hotel across from the Burbank airport. There are riots, guns going off, tables being turned over, etc. There are three cameras going. Max has no idea what's happening, and at the end of a total mess, he yells, "Cut! Print! I don't know what we got but we must have gotten something." Actually, we got nothing.

Corey Allen comes back to do two shows. He promises he'll do them on time. We have a big warehouse we're going to film in.

"John, if you can get that warehouse open for me Saturday and Sunday, by the time the crew gets here on Monday, I can give you the setup and the first five or six shots."

"That'll be great, Corey."

We make arrangements and get him in the warehouse. We all show up Monday. "Okay, Corey, what's the first shot?"

"I don't know."

"You don't know? You've been here for two days, and you don't know?"

"Well, I'll have it figured out in a few minutes."

It took him one hour.

John LaBerti was the assistant director on *Whiz Kids*. He probably suffered the most. On a Saturday night Corey would call him around eleven o'clock. "We have forty extras in Monday's scene. Change the count. Instead of twenty girls and twenty boys, change it to thirty-four girls and six boys. I want sixteen of the girls to be carrying yellow pencils, the others to be carrying ballpoint pens, and all the boys to be carrying yellow-lined pads. That's all very important." Coreyisms like that didn't pick us up any rating points.

Sometimes driving around in the van with Corey, looking for locations, I'd start feeling optimistic. He'd be riding in the front seat, and I'd be behind him with the other people involved in the show. I'd be thinking that Corey, since he has the script out, is preparing. One day I mention this to our driver, Dana Crocker.

"What do you mean, preparing? He's asleep."

That's the way things went on *Whiz Kids*. Phil was way ahead of his time with the whole computer aspect to the show, but unfortunately *Whiz Kids* was not well received. The kids solved the crimes, but they couldn't solve the Nielsen ratings. The show was cancelled after the second season.

DON BELLISARIO: A COMPLICATED GENIUS

The first pilot I did at Universal was called *Tales of the Brass Monkey*. This was in 1981, right after I finished *Gangster Chronicles* and before *Simon & Simon* resumed production. (I just wanted to get *Whiz Kids* out of the way!) The executive producer on the show was Don Bellisario who was absolutely one of the most brilliant men I've ever met. Don is still very active today. He was the producer of *Magnum P.I.* and *Quantum Leap* and later did one of the most successful shows on television, *JAG*.

At this time the studio felt that *Simon & Simon* wouldn't be picked up. The idea was that I would do the *Brass Monkey* pilot and then continue on as a producer. The script was absolutely the best script I'd ever been given. Then, of course, the dreaded network got involved.

The show took place pre–World War II. It was about two guys flying a small cargo plane, the Goose, in the Pacific. Stephen Collins played the lead airplane pilot, and Jeff MacKay was his copilot. Jeff's character had a drinking problem, which at the time was very interesting for a TV show. The network, ABC, thought not. "We can't have a guy on week after week who keeps drinking. We're probably going to put this show on at eight o'clock at night. We simply can't do that."

What we settled for was a character who had a chocolate problem. We were going to put on the first chocoholic on TV, and believe me, the last.

Every director in Hollywood wanted to direct this show. Don narrowed the choice down to two directors: Ray Austin and Alan Levi, both of whom I had worked with on *Simon & Simon*. They both wanted it very badly. The choice finally was Ray Austin because he had done a lot more action than Levi, and we thought that he would be right for it.

We're in preparation for the pilot. We have to shoot the show with the Goose, which is a little plane that can carry at most four people with light cargo. In the script we have a big storm, which is the climax of the show. Bellisario calls me into the office.

"John, I've got this great idea. I talked with Davy Jones, our pilot, who's gonna be doing all of our second unit stuff. He and I have worked this out, and I know you're gonna be happy. We're gonna do something that's never been done before. We're not gonna have one of these phony storms shot in process. Davy says that he can actually find a real storm. We're going to shoot this pilot in Hawaii. Davy will find a real storm, and what we'll do is film the scene in a real storm. It will be the first time this has ever been done! How does that grab you?"

Now when you're put in a situation like that, you don't know whether the guy is putting you on, whether he wants to start trouble, or whether he actually thinks this could be done. I say, "Don, we're going to have sound in this scene."

"Of course."

"We have six actors and a dog in the scene, right?"

"Right."

"We're going to photograph it. We're going to have sound, and obviously we're not going to get everything on the first take. We'll need coverage. We'll need makeup and hair…that's more people than the Goose holds. It's a great idea if only Stephen Collins is in the plane. Otherwise, I don't see how we can do it."

"Is this the way it's gonna be? Are you just gonna say no to everything?"

"Don, if you can work it out, fine. Just change the script!"

We wound up shooting in process.

Two days later I'm in Bellisario's office. "John, I know you're gonna be excited about this. I've hired a group of mimes to play the stunt people on the island." We had a bunch of animals on the island to attack the heroes. "You know mimes can move more like animals than any stunt people in animal costumes. They're all signed."

"Could I just ask for one thing, Don? If you don't want to use stunt people, that's fine. But remember, these mimes have to take shots, fall out of trees, and basically do what stunt people do. They're not going to be drawing windows and making funny faces."

"What do you mean?"

"Mimes are fine with me, but all I want is a couple of days to shoot tests. Just let me have two of the mimes come in and do tests. If they can take a fall, that's great. I agree with you; you're absolutely right. They certainly can move more like animals than any stunt person we could get."

We tested the two mimes. You can imagine how the tests turned out. One of the mimes wouldn't even attempt to jump out of a tree. The other mime was on a very low branch, jumped about three feet, and didn't land properly. We wound up using all stunt people. To this day I wonder if Don was trying to test me, or if he really hoped these things would work.

No question, Don was absolutely brilliant. He was also stubborn. He loved to cause chaos. A number of producers, as well as a number of executives in every business, seem to feel that their projects are going best when there is utter chaos. The more chaos Don could cause, the better he liked it.

We get the cast together and get ready to start filming in Hawaii. I pick out one of the locations and show it to Don and Ray. They decide to pick their own locations. Naturally they choose places we can't get the equipment to. It would have taken five or six days just to get the equipment in.

We wind up shooting on Oahu. We're in Oahu during the only period in years when they have a cold spell. Now, *Brass Monkey* is a show based in the tropical islands where people are getting off planes saying lines like, "Oh my God, it's so hot here, so hot!" As they're saying this, you can see the actors' breaths coming out of their mouths like smoke. That's how cold it is. It's so cold they actually run out of blankets on Oahu. The whole crew and cast are freezing the entire time.

Don is mad. "John, we haven't got quite what I wanted to get. We're staying here for another week."

He tells me this on the last day of filming in Hawaii. It's a Saturday morning, and the crew is set to depart at five o'clock that afternoon. "Don, we have a weather report. It's supposed to be like this for the next ten days."

"I don't care what the weather report is."

"Well, I'll tell you what, call Bob Harris [head of Universal television at the time], and if Bob Harris tells me to stay, we'll stay; otherwise, we go."

The crew is divided. A lot of the crew worked for Don and would continue to do so. On the other hand, they know I'm in charge of getting this show done. I learned right then that confronting Don Bellisario in front of a number of people might win you the battle but would lose you the war. I won the battle. We left that afternoon, and that was the last time that Don Bellisario ever spoke to me.

When the show went to series, the title changed from *Tales of the Brass Monkey* to *Tales of the Gold Monkey*. I was not asked to produce the show.

THE NONUNION EXPERIENCE

*M*uch later I did another pilot at Universal called *The Men*, a heavy drama about a group of close male friends trying to make a go of it. This show was done during the Writers Guild strike in 1988. It featured

Ving Rhames, who became a major star in both films and television. The writer-producer who created the show was Steve Brown. The director was Peter Werner, one of the most talented directors I ever worked with. As we began production, the Writers Guild strike was pending. If the strike occurred, it was going to cause us all kinds of difficulties.

Universal had decided to shoot the pilot under the banner of Chuck Sellier Productions. This was a nonunion operation. It was also a one-man operation. Chuck Sellier was a very interesting person. He did things in strange ways, but he probably knew as much about every area of the business as anyone. Chuck had his own crew. He was able to hire a lot of young kids who'd work for him for starvation wages just to learn the business. No one on the crew could do anything unless Chuck okayed it. He had three people who were great. They did everything.

What happened working with Chuck's nonunion crew was that instead of one electrician for every lamp being paid a considerable amount of money, plus overtime and meal penalties, his nonunion crew had four people on every lamp who were each paid just $200 a week. No fringe benefits. No health or welfare. No pension. No meal penalties. No overtime. Twenty-four hours a day, and seven days a week. To Sellier's company, time wasn't money; the only thing that was money was money.

We started filming in Baltimore, Maryland, which is a right-to-do-business state. We had a setup in a bar with a parking lot right across the street. I figured Chuck would set the generator in the parking lot and run the cable to the bar. It would take twenty-five minutes to lay the cable, and we'd be ready to shoot. I got there at 5:00 a.m. and looked for the crew. They weren't there. I looked and looked and looked. I finally found them a half mile down the street, starting to lay the cable. Chuck explained to me why the crew call, instead of being 7:30 a.m. for 8:00 a.m., was 5:00 a.m. for 8:00 a.m. The parking lot across from the bar wanted $500 for the day. The parking lot that Chuck found wanted $50 a day. Since hours meant nothing to Chuck, but money did, the crew spent three hours laying the cable. Everything in the production went that way.

We were working with nonunion drivers. Chuck Sellier's crew was mostly from Oregon, Arizona, and Utah. They had never been to Baltimore. We had to make moves from one location to another. The drivers had no idea how to get to the next location. What would normally be a ten-minute move would take a good two hours. Everybody was pulling out their handmade maps and trying to find the locations.

The most important person on Chuck's crew was the craft service person. In nonunion shows, that person is always one of the most important people on the crew. He must not only clean up, but he must be a magnificent chef. Since the crew does not have meal penalties, a lunch or dinner break is rarely called. What happens is that there's always food being passed around. The food is gourmet-style and always available. The crew works eighteen to twenty hours a day, but no one ever goes to sleep hungry.

The Writers Guild strike hit us just before we started filming in Baltimore. It was really a tough shoot. What happens during a Writers Guild strike with the writer-producer on the set? The writer can't write. If somebody offers changes, he can say, "Yes, I think that's good" or "No, I don't think that's good." He can't say, "Why don't you say this instead of that or that instead of this?" These constraints put Steve in a very difficult spot.

Of course, when a tough situation like this arises in Hollywood, everyone jumps on the bandwagon and becomes a writer. Kerry Mc-Cluggage was in charge of Universal television at this time. He always had notes on dialogue changes. Charmaine Ballion was the Universal rep who would visit us from time to time in Baltimore with Kerry's changes. If Steve said he didn't like Kerry's changes, Charmaine would get upset. We'd have to calm her down. "Look, Steve does have the right to say 'yes' or 'no' as he's the producer and the creator of the show."

In Baltimore they didn't know what title to give me. They couldn't call me the producer. Chuck Sellier was the producer. Since it was a nonunion show, Universal could only be the distributor. Finally, they settled on a title: the "distributor's representative." I forgot my title from time to time and said a number of things about production. If something came up productionwise, I'd chime right in—often in front of the representative from the Baltimore Film Commission.

"For somebody who's a distributor's representative, you seem to know a lot about production."

"Well, I've been on a lot of sets."

Amazingly, not only did we get the show made, it was also sold.

My favorite statement in life is this: "It's better to be lucky than to be smart." After wrapping up *The Men*, I was thinking about what I would like to do next. I remembered that when *Simon & Simon* ended, Gerald McRaney would still have thirteen on-air shows guaranteed in his contract. An idea suddenly hit me: "I'll come up with a show for Gerald!"

I FINALLY SELL A SHOW: *MAJOR DAD*

$\mathscr{D}$uring my career at Universal, I'd had numerous ideas for shows. I would go up and present them.

"That's wonderful, John. But we really like what you're doing, and we want you to keep doing it. But any ideas you have, always bring them to us." If I'd thought of the idea for *Friends*, they would have never bought it. Maybe I was going about things the wrong way.

I came up with an idea for Gerald. McRaney loved the service. I had him playing a Marine Major who had just been widowed. He had to come back to the States and raise three daughters. He became involved with a bunch of paperwork, doing stuff he hadn't done in years and wasn't accustomed to doing because he had been a real Marine hero during the Vietnam War. He had been overseas most of the time his daughters were growing up.

I called Rick Okie, who was a writer-producer of *Simon* at the time and a friend of mine, and told him my idea.

"Could I write this with you?"

"Sure."

We wrote it up, and I would say, at the most, it took us an hour and a half. We got it to the Writers Guild of America and registered it. This was the beginning of *Major Dad*.

At last I used my head. "Rick, instead of going to the people at Universal and telling them the idea, why don't we go to Michael Karg, Gerald's agent, and tell him about it? Then we can have a meeting with Gerald."

We find Michael Karg, who happens to be on the lot that day. "This is the greatest idea ever, and Mackey is going to love it. Let's go see him in his motor home right away."

We go talk to Gerald. "I love it. Let's do it."

Michael Karg's persistence paid off. If it wasn't for him, the show would have never seen the light of day.

"I'm gonna set up a meeting with Kerry McCluggage and Dick Lindheim. We're gonna get this going."

Three days later we have our meeting. Kerry was impressed. "This sounds great. We want to do something with it. We have to call our syndication department and find out their thoughts. We'll get back to you."

He calls us an hour later. "Syndication loves it! Let's have another meeting this Friday night."

At this meeting we're introduced to Earl Pomerantz. Kerry tells us that we need somebody who has a name in comedy. Now, what I have in mind for this show is to do it like *M*A*S*H*. Shoot it with one camera, use locations, and do it in a manner that honors the military. Nobody has said anything about doing a three-camera show in front of an audience with a laugh track. But even though the show really isn't a sitcom, it's comedy, and Earl has a big name with the networks.

We're all talking. Kerry decides to go. "I'll leave you guys here to work things out."

Pomerantz looks up. "Well, I've got a lot of ideas about this show. I don't want him in the military. I don't really care for the military. I want him to be a college professor or maybe even a journalist, but definitely not in the military."

"Really?"

"I hear, John, that they like you in the tower so I guess that I'm gonna be stuck with you guys."

"You're gonna be stuck with us? How about us being stuck with you?"

We did not get off to the world's best start.

On Monday morning I call Lindheim and tell him that no way am I or McRaney going to do this show unless it's going to be about the military. Lindheim says he'll straighten that out, which he does. We then get into starting to pitch the show to a network. The first network we go to is ABC. Brandon Stoddard was in charge at the time. We hold a pre-pitch meeting in Kerry McCluggage's office.

"You say this, I'll say that, you say this, I'll say that. This is the way it'll work." It all sounds fine.

We go over to ABC with a total of twelve people. This is our first mistake. Twelve of us to two of them. Brandon does not like the military or the idea for the show, but Gerald is a hot property. As Brandon begins to question us, he starts to bait Gerald. Gerald takes the bait. By the time Gerald is finished, all of the comedy aspects of the show are gone. We leave knowing we've struck out. ABC calls that afternoon. "We love McRaney, but we hate the project."

Next we call NBC. They aren't interested in a meeting. Then we try CBS, which at the time is in third place in the ratings. They're very interested.

We have our meeting at CBS. We cut our pitch group down from twelve people to four. We meet with Kim Lemaster and Barbara Corday, who were the two people in charge of CBS at the time. This was the only time they were together in a meeting the whole time I worked with them.

"This sounds really good. Let us think about it, and we'll set up another meeting." This is the normal thing that is done: "We'll talk to our people." Of course, that's the line all people at the networks use. (With producers, it's "I like you, but I don't know if they'll like you." Does anyone know who "our people" are, or who "they" are?)

We go back to CBS the next week. Barbara Corday says, "Look, we want to do this show, but we have one big change. There are too many shows with widowers. Let's do it differently. Let's have him fall in love with a widow. She'll have three daughters. We'll have him marry her in show number four." We decide to think about it.

Gerald is dead set against it, as is his agent. There's a stigma attached to the word "stepfather." All of us are against the idea except for Pomerantz, who is noncommittal. Kerry calls us. "Look, if you want a show, we're gonna have to do it their way; otherwise there's no way."

We give in. "It's going to be a good show. We'll do it."

CBS is delighted. Then we go back for our final meeting to get things set up. We need to figure out the pilot script. At this point, Barbara Corday tells me some things I've never heard of before. "Kim's not here, so I'll answer the questions. If I'm not here, Kim will answer the questions."

This was great, for them. Kim could say, "Oh, I've gotta check this out with Barbara." Barbara could say, "I've gotta check this out with Kim." Or Barbara would ask, "Well, does Kim know about this?" Or Kim would ask, "Does Barbara know about this?" After a while, I began to wonder if it would ever be possible for the two of them to be present at the same meeting. Wishful thinking.

Barbara informs me at this meeting that the show is going to be a three-camera show. There goes my participation. I've never produced a three-camera show. I know it will be joke after joke after joke. Then Barbara tells me that the show will be done on tape.

"Why on tape?"

"John, when people see a show on tape, right away they know it's funny, and they start to laugh."

"Really. That's interesting. I've been in the business for years. Maybe I'm just stupid, but I couldn't tell you whether a show is on tape or on film, the way it comes over on the TV screen."

"No, no, the people can tell, John. You just don't understand."

"Okay, Barbara. The three-camera is fine. There's no way that we're doing it on tape, we're going to do it on film, period."

Barbara didn't smile, but Gerald backed me.

THE SITCOM WORLD OF TODAY: NOT DESI'S OR LUCY'S

*C*arl, Rick, and I got together to figure out who was going to do what. We then set to work on the script, getting locations, and building the sets. I went down to Camp Pendleton Marine Base to match the sets with the way things were at Pendleton. Rick and Earl worked on this script. I didn't understand the jokes. Rick didn't either, but he tried to be supportive of Earl.

We found out about Earl's background as a sitcom writer. His biggest credit was writing the dialogue for Marilu Henner's character in *Taxi*. We found out that the way most sitcoms were being done was that each writer was assigned a character to write for. I had never heard of this before. The most successful TV sitcom I was familiar with was *I Love Lucy*. They did thirty-nine shows a year and took one break of two weeks. They had two writers, Bob Carroll and Madelyn Pugh, and a writer-producer, Jess Oppenheimer. That was it. Desi Arnaz was the executive producer. There was no special writer for Lucy, Desi, Bill Frawley, Vivian Vance, or any of the guest stars.

The way *Major Dad* was set up after the pilot was sold was this: we would do three shows, take a two-week break, do three shows, take a two-week break, and so on. This was for twenty-four shows.

I get back from Camp Pendleton, and we start building the sets and doing the casting. When the sets have been built, I encounter the real world of sitcoms, courtesy of Earl Pomerantz. Earl comes down to the set to look things over. "Just a minute. You've got all these walls khaki-colored."

"That's right, I do."

"Well, khaki isn't funny."

"What do you mean, it isn't funny?"

"John, people don't look at khaki walls and start to laugh."

"What about the audience? Aren't they supposed to laugh?"

"You don't get it. The audience won't laugh at khaki walls."

"What color will they laugh at, Earl?"

"Yellow. When people see yellow walls, they start laughing."

"Earl, at Camp Pendleton they don't have yellow . . . oh, never mind."

Earl continues. "John, those numbers that you have on the doors—202, 203, that's not funny."

"What do you mean, that's not funny?"

"John, the number should be eight; you hear the number eight, and you start to laugh."

I'm not exaggerating. This was the exact conversation. I started to realize that I was in the wrong place at the wrong time. I had created a show but I couldn't see myself lasting with it.

Then, all of a sudden, more bad news. Will McKenzie was hired as the director. Will McKenzie knew the few things in the world that Gerald McRaney didn't know. He started changing everything. The worst change was making the characters into caricatures. The show became a total insult to the military. The worst change of all was to Gerald McRaney's character. Instead of being a lovable fellow with a lot of strength, he wound up being a brutal Sgt. Markoff type (the Brian Donlevy part in *Beau Geste*).

We went into casting. The main part we were looking for was the girl who eventually would be Gerald's wife. We saw forty to fifty girls. We settled on Shanna Reed. She was a good actress and very professional. After the marriage, her parts kept getting smaller. She stood up for certain ideas and values. The producers didn't like that.

As we started to shoot the pilot, I found myself becoming more and more disenchanted with the whole thing.

We finished the pilot. The show was sold. It had pretty good success the first season. In its second season, *Major Dad* shot up into the top ten. That was good and bad. The good was being in the top ten. Everybody was watching the show for one simple reason: the United States was in the Gulf War at the time, and every episode was about the war. The bad news was that in reruns the show would become immediately dated. Universal would be left with one whole season becoming obsolete in syndication. *Major Dad* ran from 1989 through 1992. The show ended after four seasons with one season being a total waste.

The hardest thing I had to do was to go to the set every Friday night and watch the filming. The money was good; the royalties and the foreign residuals were fine. The residuals from the United States were nothing to sneeze at either. My role, like Shanna Reed's, became smaller and smaller. One night I finally pulled another of my many famous mistakes. I was getting more and more upset with the whole Pomerantz group and everything they were doing. They were upset with me, probably rightfully so. They decide to fire the warm-up man. That's the fellow who, when a sitcom is filmed in front of a live studio audience, comes out, tells some jokes, and gets the audience in the mood to laugh.

Earl Pomerantz comes to me before the show. "I want you to fire him, John." The reason Earl wanted him fired was that he wanted to do the warm-ups himself.

"Fine, Earl, I'll fire him."

I liked the guy who was doing the warm-ups. I go to him before the show and tell him that this is going to be his last warm-up. You can imagine how this goes over. He comes out to do the warm-up and insults everybody in the entire company. By the time he finishes, the audience is in shock. The show lays an egg.

I left *Major Dad* that night. I'm probably the only creator-producer to leave his own show.

Here's what would happen with Universal television shows. Universal would pay people what it owed them when the show went into syndication. Here's the trick. The company sold *Major Dad* to USA cable network, which it owned jointly with Paramount at the time. It did this instead of trying to shop the show elsewhere, where there would have been a lot more money for the participants. Universal figured it might need McRaney and Pomerantz at some point, so it gave them the money they were due. Rick Okie and I were given nothing. Another frequent occurrence on Universal shows was the filing of a lawsuit by those people Universal figured they could do without.

It's extremely difficult to sue a studio like Universal. Any lawyer who's a show biz lawyer is on retainer to Universal. The company has lawyers in Los Angeles, Chicago, New York, and any place you'd turn (maybe not Kanab). Lawyers kept turning our case down because it would have been a conflict of interest. Rick and I finally found a lawyer named Joe Hart in Beverly Hills, of all places. He was not on retainer to Universal. We settled out of court for eighty percent of what was due to us. Neither of us complained.

Since I own ten percent of *Major Dad*, I still get a statement every year from Universal. As of my last statement, the show is only sixty-eight million dollars in arrears. All of Universal bookkeeping is based on interest rates. The interest rates at the time the show was made were between nine percent and ten percent. Universal always showed a loss on their books for each show every season. The company figured out how much money you'd lost for it, then how much money it would make if it invested these losses at ten percent. The interest is then compounded daily. After much soul-searching, I decided not to write a check to Universal for the $6,800,000 to square my ten percent.

I BECOME A PITCHMAN AND STRIKE OUT

*W*hy did Universal let me go at the end of my last contract? I knew why. Here was a producer who wouldn't let any of the people from the tower go on to our set, except obviously for Robert Harris or Dick Lindheim. None of their subordinates were allowed to go on the sets unless they checked it out with me first. If they did, they would always cause trouble. Now, years later, I can understand their feelings. Take a young person in their twenties, on their way up the ladder. Every Monday morning there's a meeting in the tower. The person assigned to *Simon & Simon* is questioned. "Well, what happened on *Simon & Simon* last week? Everything going all right there?"

"I don't know, I'm not allowed on the set by the producer."

I understand their point, but my point was that this was the only way I could get things done.

They never threw me a going-away party.

Strangely enough, after leaving Universal, I wound up doing my very next show for Universal syndication the following year. It was called *Strays*. They had been filming and were in a lot of trouble after four or five days. I got a phone call from Angela McPherson, who was in charge of production for Universal syndication.

"John, can you come in and finish this show? I'll send you the script."

It was an excellent script by Shaun Cassidy about a young married couple who move into an isolated farmhouse with their five-year-old daughter and are terrorized by hundreds of stray cats. The stars were the fellow from *thirtysomething*, Timothy Busfield, an Emmy winner, and Kathleen Quinlan, later an Academy Award nominee for *Apollo 13*. John McPherson, who happened to be married to Angela McPherson, was the director. John had worked as the director of photography on *Gangster Chronicles*. Niki Marvin was the executive producer. She went on to be nominated for an Academy Award for producing *The Shawshank Redemption*.

The first night I go on location—the whole show was shot night for night—everybody gathers around me, very frightened. They all expect to be fired. I give one of my shorter speeches.

"No one's getting fired."

I figured that if the people on the crew were doing a bad job, I'd try to help them any way that I could. Bringing in a whole new crew would be time-consuming to say the least.

The people who owned the property couldn't understand why we were filming there. The company had built an entire house from scratch on location, including the exteriors and the interiors. All of the filming in the house was night for night. The director insisted on not scrimming the windows, that is, not closing off the windows. This forced us to shoot night for night instead of day for night. Out in the middle of nowhere, this made no sense at all. All they had to do was tarp the windows, and it would look like night. If you're shooting inside of a house that is in a deserted area, you can't see anything outside the windows at night anyway. We lost four hours of filming a day shooting this way. At night we'd call dinner for thirty minutes. The only place we could feed everyone was thirty minutes away by bus. We lost an hour and a half each night.

We finally finished filming outside. The last day we're shooting inside a warehouse. I look over the schedule and see that we have "poor man's process." That's people seated in a car when the car isn't moving. It's a night scene, so naturally I assume that the car will be put in front of a wall on a stage. Much too sensible. They're going to shoot the scene night for night, outside.

I go to the assistant director. "Why are you shooting this outside at night? You don't see anything."

"Because the script says 'outside.'" He's not kidding!

"Guys, all you do is put the car inside. We put the car in front of a wall, and it's the exact same shot. Why bother to wait until nighttime to shoot this?"

"You think that'll work?"

"Yeah, I really think it will."

After *Strays*, I decided to try to come up with some ideas of my own. I'd work with writers and go to pitch meetings. At this time a whole new breed had moved into the syndicated market. My agent, Irv Schecter, would set up a meeting with me and the writers to go pitch a show. We'd go in. There'd be the usual ten minutes of baseball talk, small talk, whatever. The people we'd meet were always very young, in their midtwenties, and after the small talk, we'd give the pitch.

"Oh, this is great. This is sensational. We've got a deal." We'd never hear from them again.

I remember my last pitch meeting at Warner Bros. I don't remember the fellow's name (probably on purpose). We arrive a bit early. I'm there with a lady from my agent's office and the writer, John Bonni. The fellow we're supposed to meet with walks by.

"Is one of you John Stephens?"

"I am."

"Oh."

He walks off. My agent turns to me. "John, do you know this guy?"

"No, I don't."

The man comes back at the time the meeting's supposed to start. "So you're John Stephens."

"Yeah."

"I hate you."

"Huh?"

"I said I hate you. I'm gonna tell you why I hate you. I was doing a show with Tim and Daphne Reid over at Universal that I was producing with a friend of mine. We had a lot of your crew there and all I'd hear from Tim Reid is 'John Stephens would never do this. J. S. wouldn't do it that way. Here's what John would do.' Then Mike Moder (the head of production at Viacom) would come down to the set saying, 'We're bringing in John Stephens who's gonna be over you. You'd better get used to that. Things are gonna start shaping up around here.' Every day, over and over again we'd keep hearing your name. Our cameraman, Lloyd Ahern, would always be bringing up your name. 'John wouldn't do this, John wouldn't do that.' I got so sick of you that when the show was cancelled, my partner and I considered getting out of the business. Now I'm back in the business, and I've gotta tell you, you almost drove me out of the business! Okay, let's hear your pitch."

Somehow the pitch lacked enthusiasm.

MY SWAN SONG

*M*y swan song was a pilot originally called *Doors* and retitled *Doorways*. This was at TriStar. For a last experience, it was an interesting one, to say the least. Peter Werner, a director with whom I'd worked before, calls me wanting to know if I'll be available to produce his pilot.

"Send me the script."

"Done."

It's a good script. There's a lot of action in it and a lot of special effects. I call Peter back and agree to do the show.

Bill Phillips was the head of TV production at TriStar. He had worked for me on *Three for the Road* as the associate producer. We never got along. Bill and I discussed the script and how we would proceed with the production. He gave me the budget. It was ludicrous. No one could come anywhere near the budget with all of the special effects involved. They had ice-covered mountains, spaceships, anything you could think of was in the script. The budget was about a million dollars short. What they wanted—all studios love to do this—was to cut $500,000 out of the budget. Knowing what studios do, I went along with it.

We start the preproduction. Peter wants a cameraman who I'd introduced him to, Neil Roach.

"Neil's not right for this show, Peter."

"Okay, but I like working with him. Who do you want?"

"All right, Peter, let's go with Neil." Big mistake.

Bill Phillips also knew Neil and was very happy with him.

We started casting the show. There were two main parts. We settled on George Newbern, who had been the bridegroom in the remake of *Father of the Bride*, as the male lead. For the girl we had a search approaching Scarlett O'Hara magnitude. It was nationwide and then became worldwide. They finally settled on a French girl, Anne Le-Guernec. She only had four things going against her. Number one, the script was in English. She could barely speak English. Number two, she was not what you'd call attractive. Number three, she did not have an hourglass figure. Number four, she was not up to the physicality that the part demanded. A gentleman at TriStar fell in love with her (professionally, that is).

"She's beautiful, she's great. We have to take her."

He convinced the other people. So, unfortunately, we signed her. I set forth on what was to be my final epic.

One of the writer-producers was a person I knew well, Jim Crocker from *Simon & Simon*. The other writer-producer was George R.R. Martin, who was very big in sci-fi. As far as the show went, the effects never worked, the acting was atrocious, and so on and so on. I decided that once it was over, I would go into teaching full time. *Doorways* was my exit from show biz. Happily it never aired; it was that bad.

However, like Michael Jordan, I tried to make a comeback. I was not as successful as Jordan. I'd go to pitch meetings. I'd get there early and talk with the secretary. She'd always offer coffee and be very nice. After a few minutes she'd say, "Mr. Stephens, he'll see you now."

I'd go in, give my pitch.

"Yes, we're gonna buy it; we'll call your agent tomorrow. By the way, could you call us back at four o'clock this afternoon? Maybe we could even make a deal this afternoon."

I'd call back. The secretary would answer. I'd tell her who it was. "John Stephens? Will he know what it's regarding?"

IN CONCLUSION

In summation, would I do it all over again? Who knows? Did I enjoy working in the business? Yes. I was very fortunate to work for the people I did. I only had a few jobs that I wasn't crazy about, and even in those jobs, I could always have fun.

As Sinatra said, "I did it my way." Maybe my way was right; maybe it was wrong. There are thirty ways of doing everything. Most importantly, you have to have a way, you have to be prepared, and in TV, as in football, you have to be prepared to call "audibles." If you don't know what an audible is, "you could look it up," as Casey Stengel would say.

There are many books written about movies and television shows that failed. Everyone, except the author, made mistakes. Remember, these books are written from the author's particular point of view. On *Cleopatra* (the Burton-Taylor version), eight different books could probably be written on what went wrong. Each book would be written from one person's point of view, pointing fingers at the other people involved.

The best example of a TV disaster was a famous Hollywood book called *Only You, Dick Daring!* which was written by Merle Miller. The book lambasted everybody at Screen Gems, Jackie Cooper, Dick Dorso, and everyone connected with the project. Miller decried how they went about systematically destroying his wonderful pilot script. It was a very funny book. I finally found someone who had been at Screen Gems at the time. I couldn't resist asking him, "Jimmy, did you read the pilot script of *Dick Daring* that Miller submitted?"

"I sure did, and it was awful. His revisions were even worse."

They knew it was awful, yet not a single person ever came out and told their version of the story. Interestingly, in the book, Miller never mentions that maybe his script wasn't all that good.

As far as people in the industry having talent or not, remember that everything you hear or read is based on someone's personal experiences and interests. For instance, if you're a casting director and you use a lot of clients from a certain agent, that agent will go around singing your praises to everyone in town. If you don't use that agent's clients, believe me, they'll try to crucify you.

Basically, show business is only different from other businesses in that there is no definite standard for good or bad. It's like art; beauty is in the eye of the beholder. Some people like something; other people don't. You're subject to the whims of the projection room and later on, the theater or TV screens. "This is good, this is terrible. This is wonderful, this stinks." In TV, you hope for one of two things: great reviews or great ratings. Sometimes the former doesn't cut it. The latter always does. You do the best you can and also have fun.

Remember, if you're a producer, you're the coach, not the quarterback. The better the quarterback, the better the team's record, and the better you look as the coach. Don't be afraid to hire talented people who are as bright or maybe brighter than you are. It only makes you look good.

Everything else will work out.

ଔ The End ଓ

Index

About the Author

John G. Stephens has worked in television for five decades as a producer, creator, casting director, production manager, and reader. He produced the successful television shows *The Millionaire*, *My Three Sons*, *Family Affair*, *Gunsmoke*, *Marciano*, *How the West Was Won*, and *Simon & Simon*. He created the series *Major Dad*. Mr. Stephens taught Producing for Television at UCLA for seven years and instructed Japanese film students on American television. He has been a guest lecturer at California State University at Northridge, California Lutheran University, and Beverly Hills High School. Mr. Stephens' broad experience and long career have made him a favorite on entertainment shows on A&E and the Biography Channel. He currently works as a television consultant.